"The decision to name a new CEO is one of the most important a company can make. With this book in hand, though, you'll be ready. Every CEO and board member should read it, heed its lessons, and put its tools into action."
Daniel H. Pink, author of *Drive* and *To Sell Is Human*

"It's hard enough to be a CEO, overseeing and guiding the complexities of the business. It's harder still to gracefully and successfully hand the reins over to your next-in-line, so they too will thrive. This playbook shares a practical and well-designed suite of tools to give everyone involved the very best chance of success."
Michael Bungay Stanier, author of *The Coaching Habit*

"CEOs often feel insecure and uncertain when their boards take the lead in succession planning (as boards should). Your CEO Succession Playbook will help CEOs get out in front and play their role in succession with finesse. This book beautifully illuminates the emotions under the surface of the succession process and suggests the mindsets and conversations the CEO can adopt to make it more successful and fulfilling."
Helen Handfield-Jones, Practice Lead, CEO Performance, WATSON; one of Canada's foremost authorities on the subjects of CEO succession planning and CEO evaluation

"The genius of this book is that its authors clearly demonstrate that the path to excellence as a CEO (and board member) is by integrating a succession process into the leadership patterns and practices of the current CEO, board members and management team. The book is not only a rich and reliable travel guide to mastering this challenging journey, but it presents well documented arguments that successful succession planning seamlessly integrates with successful CEO performance. Read this book to be

a better CEO, read it to be a better board member, read it to be a better CEO candidate, read it to be a better business student."
Walt Sutton, entrepreneur, CEO, CEO coach and author of *Leap of Strength* and *The Mingus Parchment*

"*Your CEO Succession Playbook* should be on any CEO's bookshelf. It hits all the key issues, from big-picture to little picture. It asks the important questions... and ones that go beyond your last day of work... like, 'Is there life after being a CEO?' This companion gets your head in a good place and provides the tools you'll need to meet all your transition objectives."
Mark Goodale, Co-founder, Morrisey Goodale LLC, a management consulting firm to the AEC industry

"A must-read for boards and CEOs—the most valuable resource I have read on the topic. It reminds us that culture and relationships are at the heart of a successful CEO transition."
Stuart Suls, President and CEO, Mr. Lube Canada

"*Your CEO Succession Playbook* is a remarkable resource that offers CEOs an impressive set of practical tools for executing the CEO succession management process. Unique in its focus on CEO incumbents and their specific needs and concerns throughout the process, this book offers a comprehensive yet incredibly accessible approach for CEOs to work collaboratively with their board members, succession committee, executive team members, senior HR leaders, and other critical stakeholders. *Your CEO Succession Playbook* is an indispensable resource for CEO succession management that will aptly serve CEO incumbents for many years to come."
Kevin Groves, Associate Professor of Organizational Theory and Management, Pepperdine University, and author of *Winning Strategies*

"A compelling read, and a must for all business leaders. While targeted at current CEOs the book is so appropriate for board directors and any prospective CEOs. A first that deals with how

to make succession planning a success. I recommend this superb toolkit as a prerequisite to ensuring sound business continuity!"
Anthony Ariganello, CPHR, FCPA, FCGA, ICD.D, President and CEO CPHR BC-YK and Canada

"This is essential reading for those committed to a successful CEO transition. It shifts the conversation from, 'What do I need to do to get CEO succession right?' to 'Who do I need to be as a leader to do this well, and avoid nasty politics?'"
Kathryn Young, Partner, Canada, Boyden Executive Search

"The book is founded on an assumption I use often, and that is that all CEOS are temporary, yet the companies they work for are enduring. Given this reality, a CEO's ultimate job is to make the company better for the time they are there, yet their legacy comes from developing the future CEO and setting them up for success. This book provides the tools and leadership insights CEOs and boards need to build a legacy around developing future CEOs, and by doing so they will build a more successful business today."
Mark Blucher, President and CEO, Insurance Corporation of British Columbia

"Ignoring the certainty that you will one day leave your CEO position does great harm, to your organization, its people and its customers. The inevitable rumors, speculation and rivalry can quickly negate years of blood sweat and tears you have invested in the business. This is easy to avoid. Simply implement the practical ideas in this fantastic book, without delay. And in the process, leave your legacy intact."
Colin Gautrey, Executive Coach and author of *Influential Leadership: A Leader's Guide to Getting Things Done*

"A valuable addition to the repertoire on CEO transitions. This book is a compendium of latest thinking on CEO succession, put into a practical framework. Written in a straightforward and practical manner, it provides CEOs with guidance, tools, and coaching on how to navigate through one of the most important yet personally difficult aspects of their tenure as CEO—preparing for a thoughtful transition."

Mathé Grenier, Senior Client Partner and member of Korn Ferry Global CEO Succession Practice

"*Your CEO Succession Playbook* provides a straightforward and practical guide to help CEOs, and their boards, prepare for their inevitable departures in timely and organized manners, and avoid the numerous pitfalls that surround the process. The book is particularly well-suited for the engineering/consulting industry, given the succession planning challenges so many firms face."

Paul Zofnass, President, Environmental Financial Consulting Group (EFCG), New York, a leading provider of business and financial management to the global AEC industry

"*Your CEO Succession Playbook* provides a succession process that creates a framework for a smooth transition in which all stakeholders win. I recommend this book to anyone who is involved in CEO succession."

George Melville, Chairman and Owner, Boston Pizza International Inc. and inductee into the BC Business Hall of Fame. Current Chancellor, Kwantlen Polytechnic University

"The title of the book says it all—great succinct read with the advice, tools and resources to successfully manage perhaps the most critical succession in a company's journey, that of the CEO."

Praveen Varshney, Director, Varshney Capital and entrepreneur, investor, long time member of Entrepreneur Organization (EO)

"This book is more than a playbook: it's a call to action. I want every CEO in Mackay CEO Forums to read it, develop others, and finish strong."

Nancy Mackay, Founder and CEO of MacKay CEO Forums, a peer group learning organization dedicated to building better leaders; co-author of *The Talent Advantage*

YOUR CEO SUCCESSION PLAYBOOK

Natalie Michael & Brian Conlin

YOUR
CEO
SUCCESSION
PLAYBOOK

HOW TO PASS THE TORCH
SO EVERYONE WINS

TRIFOLD

Trifold Publishing
Vancouver BC
www.YourCEOSuccessionPlaybook.com

Cataloguing data available from Library and Archives Canada
. ISBN 978-0-9959958-0-2 (paperback)
ISBN 978-0-9959958-1-9 (ebook)

Produced by Page Two
www.pagetwostrategies.com
Cover and interior design by Peter Cocking
17 18 19 20 21   5 4 3 2 1

This book is dedicated to all the CEOs who wake up every day and strive to make a positive difference in the world.

Contents

INTRODUCTION

CEOS ON the whole are talented, highly motivated, successful individuals. They love a challenge and strive to achieve. But one area routinely gets swept under the rug: CEO succession.

Here are some facts. Despite the reality that every CEO will leave his or her job eventually, only two-thirds of companies have a formal CEO succession process in place. The real clincher: the majority of companies who have a CEO succession process are disappointed with the results (Björnberg and Feser, 2015).

This prompts the question: why do CEOs tolerate such dismal results at the end of their tenure? Obviously, if you are reading this book, you don't want this to happen to you! This book will help you beat the odds.

In this book we will get you ready to design and implement a CEO succession process that draws out the potential in others and leads to lasting high performance in your business. If you have attempted this before, we will show you there is a better way—one that doesn't require you to work harder and faster but, rather, more intentionally.

This book will tune your political radar so that instead of getting bogged down by the politics that often derail the CEO succession process, you can adapt your leadership approach and style to avoid political pitfalls. If you're not careful, CEO succession can quickly become "the survival of the fittest" as people make ego plays and compete for status and power. This can happen fast, leaving you wondering: what just happened here? Consider this book your strategic companion from the start of the process right through to the hand-off, making sure you stay above the fray.

In addition to helping you achieve a smooth hand-off, this book will help you figure out what to do next. We address the big question: is there life after being a CEO? In short, the answer is yes! We will give you valuable insights and practical strategies to help you start your new life chapter and avoid jumping into your "next thing" in a knee-jerk reaction. Ultimately, we hope this book provides you with a game plan to pass your torch so that everyone wins.

How This Book Came to Be

We first had the idea for this book over a smoothie at the Fairmont Waterfront Hotel in Vancouver, Canada. We were perplexed: why are all the reports on the topic of CEO succession so depressing? Do all CEOs do such a bad job at this? There must be some success stories, surely, we thought. This was the start of our mission.

We interviewed thirty-two CEOs, many of whom successfully developed and promoted their successor, while others we spoke to were newly promoted CEOs who had moved up through the ranks. For several companies, we interviewed both the former CEO and the current CEO to learn their different perspectives on the transition process. Our goal was to discover what they felt they did right and what they would do differently if faced with this again, so we could share their insights and create a CEO succession toolkit that works.

The CEOs we spoke to either lead or used to lead public, private and owner-operated companies, ranging from startups (revenue under $15 million) to large global businesses (revenues up to $3 billion). In almost all cases the outgoing CEO promoted a first-time CEO or someone with limited experience as a CEO and had the satisfaction of seeing the candidate thrive.

It is noteworthy that every CEO we approached was keen to share. Obviously, transitioning into, or out of, a CEO role doesn't happen to people every day. It represents a turning point for everyone involved. It's significant. As you go through this book, you will hear their stories—what they went through and what the experience felt like for them—and you will learn from their candor, wisdom and hard knocks. As a bit of a surprise to us, the CEOs we spoke to were delightfully candid.

To speed up your efforts, this book will provide you with a CEO succession toolkit. Here we use the word "toolkit" to mean a collection of resources, tools, advice and insights that you can adapt to your own situation and business. It includes:

- a step-by-step CEO succession process that will stand up to board scrutiny
- an overview of roles—who does what
- a sample CEO success profile including criteria for top-performing CEOs
- a definition of "CEO potential" and how to apply it
- tips for managing a candidate's expectations and how to avoid political pitfalls
- a menu of options for developing CEO candidates
- tips for designing a credible CEO selection process
- proven strategies for launching the new CEO
- a sample communication when announcing the next CEO
- practical tips for making sure that ego dynamics don't override your best-laid plans
- a framework for thinking about your own "next launch" when you leave the organization

Throughout the toolkit are key leadership techniques—how you can bring out the best in people and how you can minimize politics. From our interviews, we discovered that successful CEO transitions are more about *how* you are leading than about following process maps.

If you want to be successful at drawing out the potential of others and achieving lasting high performance in your business, then you will need to embody leadership qualities that assist others to develop and grow. Qualities like being visionary, proactive and respectful—the exact opposite of the antiquated command-and-control style from years ago. Think of this idea as similar to computers. With computers, you need the hardware to make your computer run, but the software is what really makes the difference. With CEO succession, the process is important, but the leadership qualities (like the software) are what really differentiate success. In each chapter, we showcase the leadership qualities needed to release potential, remove political interference and encourage meaningful dialogue.

Throughout the book, you will find self-coaching questions that have been provided to help you think more deeply about the content and how it applies to your situation. We anticipate that these questions will inspire you to embrace coaching as a building block for developing yourself and others. The questions also will help you link your own strategic agenda and performance outcomes to each topic area. We share additional tools online at www.YourCEOSuccession Playbook.com.

In the spirit of transparency, we want to put our bias on the table: both of us are executive coaches. Natalie is an executive coach with fifteen years of experience coaching CEOs, executives and high-capacity leaders who want to make a significant contribution in organizations and pursue meaningful careers. Brian, since stepping down as President and CEO of Golder Associates Corp., has pursued his passion for developing and coaching CEOs and executives, something he enjoyed throughout his career. We both believe in the power of coaching.

Our hope is that, as a result of picking up this book, you are able to lead a CEO transition that moves beyond the classic replacement mindset to one that is more developmental, leads to business success and sustainability and creates a framework for a smooth transition in which all stakeholders win—including you. We also hope that the self-coaching questions and insights from this book will help you to become a better leader and internal coach. In our view, coaching is a key element in bridging the gap between success and failure in this endeavor.

Who This Book Is For

We have positioned the book to speak directly to CEOs who are currently in the role and are key stakeholders in the CEO succession process. However, anyone involved in CEO succession will benefit from the insights shared and the toolkit provided. This would include board members, incoming CEOs, Human Resources executives and high-potential candidates.

How the Book Is Organized

The book is organized into six chapters to align with the six phases of a typical CEO succession process, which are noted in the figure facing. We present both the process (doing) and the leadership qualities (being) for each step along the way, showcasing how the two work together to create success.

Six-Phase CEO Succession Process

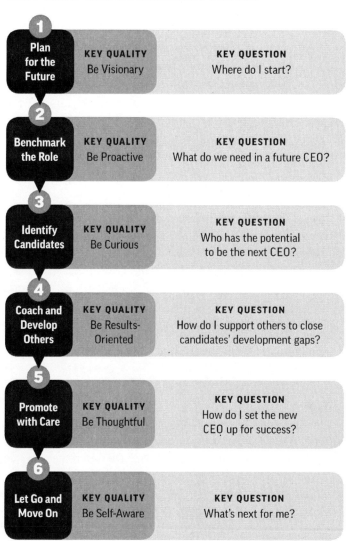

	KEY QUALITY	KEY QUESTION
1 Plan for the Future	Be Visionary	Where do I start?
2 Benchmark the Role	Be Proactive	What do we need in a future CEO?
3 Identify Candidates	Be Curious	Who has the potential to be the next CEO?
4 Coach and Develop Others	Be Results-Oriented	How do I support others to close candidates' development gaps?
5 Promote with Care	Be Thoughtful	How do I set the new CEO up for success?
6 Let Go and Move On	Be Self-Aware	What's next for me?

At the end of each chapter, we round out your succession toolkit with communication tips, political pitfalls to watch for and self-coaching questions.

Keep in mind that we have written the book in a logical sequence following the steps in a common succession process, but realistically CEO succession is much more dynamic, with many twists and turns. Frankly, when the politics emerge, it can be anything but logical!

Following is an overview of each chapter and the particular phase of planning for CEO succession that each chapter addresses.

Phase 1: Plan for the Future (Chapter 1)

Where do you start? This chapter addresses the importance of rooting your CEO succession process in a compelling vision for your company and for the CEO transition itself. Being visionary is the key leadership quality here: pushing others to think about tomorrow rather than today and pushing yourself to think about a future that extends beyond you. Being haphazard in your approach is the political pitfall that can have significant consequences down the road.

Phase 2: Benchmark the Role (Chapter 2)

What do you need in a future CEO? Here we encourage you to create a CEO success profile that works for the future. A CEO success profile helps you to benchmark candidates, communicate expectations and identify development gaps. We also share research on what distinguishes world-class CEOs and we give you a sample profile.

Being proactive is the key leadership quality: consider what will drive your company's competitive differentiation and how this affects the skills and attributes you will need in a future CEO. You also need to be proactive about managing your own potential discomfort as you talk about what is needed in a future CEO. Insecurity is the political pitfall we explore.

Phase 3: Identify Candidates (Chapter 3)

Who has the potential to be the next CEO? This chapter outlines different succession scenarios that you will need to manage, ranging from planned transitions to emergencies. For your toolkit, you'll receive a model of employee potential based on some of the latest research in this area, as well as valuable tips on how to get the most out of executive leadership assessments.

Being curious is the key leadership quality that matters here. People need to feel heard and valued; they need to know they can speak frankly with you. Without this, you will likely turn up the political heat, increasing your chances of getting burned.

Phase 4: Coach and Develop Others (Chapter 4)

What's the best way to develop future CEOs? In this chapter we share the formative experiences that the CEOs we interviewed found most valuable and we offer a menu of options for developing your CEO candidates. As in all areas of a CEO's responsibility, it is important here to have the key leadership quality of being results-oriented. You will achieve the best results when people have a development plan and there is an expectation that they will follow through. All sound good? Perhaps, but only until others perceive favoritism, the political pitfall that can stir things up.

Phase 5: Promote with Care (Chapter 5)

Who will be selected as the next CEO? How do you set them up for success? We will clarify your role, the board's critical responsibility in selection and what it truly means to set up a newly promoted CEO for success. Being thoughtful is the key leadership quality here. There is a lot to be thoughtful about: the dynamics of winners and losers in the selection process, ego defense strategies, getting out of the way and genuinely showing confidence in the incoming CEO and the future of the business.

Phase 6: Let Go and Move On (Chapter 6)

What's next for you? This chapter prepares you to leave the CEO seat and start a new career chapter. It walks you through a four-stage process we refer to as the "4R" model, which shows the predictable emotions and experiences that accompany a transition. Most importantly, we share CEO stories that highlight what it is *really like* to go through these stages. Being self-aware is the key leadership quality that helps departing CEOs update their personal narrative, move through their transition and find new threads of meaning.

A Note about the CEOs' Stories

When sharing the specific stories of the CEOs we interviewed for this book, we've opted not to identify the individuals or their companies. We believe this approach respects the candor and the sharing of emotions central to the book and that it maintains confidentiality, especially when there were discrepancies between stories from the incoming and outgoing CEOs—and sometimes there were. We have sometimes changed gender and industry; otherwise the stories are true and happened just as we describe them.

Although you may be tempted to gloss over the CEO stories, we feel it is important for you to read them attentively, as we believe in the value of learning from your peers. The CEOs we interviewed have personally undergone a CEO transition, and what they have learned during the process could very well be invaluable to you.

1

BE
VISIONARY:
PLAN FOR
THE FUTURE

Key Leadership Quality

Be visionary. Plan for the future. Get everyone involved in looking at the horizon and thinking about the future. Integrate the strategic vision with succession planning.

Near the end of a regular board meeting, the board chair asked for my thoughts on my tenure. The question caught me off guard. I thought to myself: Is [his] real question "When are you leaving?" I knew I was not prepared for that question and I despise being unprepared, especially in front of the board!

T
HE PACE of innovation in the world is impressive: robotics, artificial intelligence, neuroscience, big data, genetics, cybersecurity—and who knows what other innovations are to come. New business models and technology are impacting almost every sector. Futurists and analysts are trying their best to predict the trends that will shape business, but it seems there is not much they can agree on, with the exception of one thing: exponential change. This is the new normal.

What does this mean for CEO succession? Foresight, strategy and vision are more important than ever. The winners of tomorrow will be the companies who have a deep capacity for adaptability. Having a CEO succession program is one way to ensure that adaptability is embedded in your company's DNA. It's one strategy for helping the company navigate a volatile and uncertain future. Preparing for different scenarios, developing leadership bench strength, having an emergency candidate, cultivating executives who can rise to adaptive challenges—these are all things you can do intentionally in the pursuit of a sustainable future. Although every business is vulnerable when the top leader changes—and a few wrong moves can jeopardize a team and culture no matter how many years it took to build—it is definitely possible to have an effective transition.

What Successful CEOs Do

Start Early

One question many CEOs have about succession is: when do I start? One piece of consistent advice from our interviews: start early. As one CEO in professional services advised, "Don't get caught. Give yourself years, not months."

There are many advantages to this. First, it allows *you* to lead the discussion by framing CEO succession as one pillar of a broader strategy for building the organization's adaptive capacity, an attempt to build up the company's ongoing resilience for the future. This frame is important because it's common for people to think that if the CEO is bringing up succession, it's because he or she is secretly planning on leaving. This raises suspicions and elicits political interference.

Secondly, it takes time to develop people. The board and other key stakeholders need sufficient time to observe how candidates navigate strategic issues, react under pressure and demonstrate their capacity to lead others. If you want to do this well, you can't do it overnight. Thirdly, starting early defuses the emotional charge associated with succession. When succession happens a crisis or under pressure from a time perspective, that reduces the odds of success. When emotions run high, decisions tend to be worse.

Here is how one CEO approached succession in his first year:

In my first year as CEO, I questioned the board as to why they hired me externally when there was a lot of talent in the organization already. To provide opportunities for others in the future and to ensure that things would be different when I left, I put together a succession briefing book for the board in my first year. In it I identified who I believed was my immediate successor, the status of each potential candidate internally and a communication strategy in the event that anything would happen to me in an emergency situation. I updated this briefing book twice per year and had a search firm on retainer so that each year we could benchmark our CEO succession pipeline to the external marketplace as well.

A second CEO explained his proactive approach:

I believe hiring C-suite executives can be challenging at the best of times, and if you must hire them under pressure when emotions are running high, it reduces the odds of success. Now I groom each of my executives to be a future CEO one day. I know they won't all want the job or be capable of it, but I want to send a clear message that I want every executive to think and act like a CEO, and I focus their development plans on building C-suite capabilities. As an upside, I have a stronger-performing executive team than at any other point in my career, and each person's ongoing executive development plan becomes the foundation for succession-planning conversations.

If you wait until the last minute or until you are encouraged by the board, you disadvantage all stakeholders. So start early and don't get caught being unprepared.

Link Succession to the Business Strategy

As the CEO, one of your key responsibilities is to generate shareholder value and return on investment; this includes people development, too. With succession planning, you generate value by turning people's potential into performance; this investment pays off when leaders deliver on results. The more you can align these efforts to your current business priorities, the greater will be your return.

One CEO looks at his succession pipeline from the lens of an investor, and he encourages his board to do the same. To do this he imagines that an investor is considering investing large sums of money in his business and weighing whether the talent pipeline is an enabler for growth or an inhibitor. He asks himself questions like:

- Will an investor view our executive leadership as a competitive differentiation?
- Will they see our talent-development process as a source of company value or as a derailer?
- Will our talent pipeline lead to optimism or pessimism about our future?

He finds that the investor lens is valuable because it creates a strategic imperative, forcing him to see the linkages between future strategy implementation and executive development. It elevates his thinking and makes it clear that building a talent pipeline for CEO succession is not "nice to have." It is an important contributor to shareholder value over the longer term.

Building on this notion, another CEO told us that it is essential to link CEO succession to ongoing competitive differentiation, yet for her, this is mostly about cultivating the leadership skills and qualities in the present that will drive company differentiation in the future. She explained:

> I have found that few companies have a strategy that really leads to a competitive advantage. They think they have it, but they really have a great operational improvement strategy. The reality is that their competitors can easily replicate the plan, so the strategy is not compelling for the long term. This makes CEO succession more difficult. Without a clear differentiation in mind, it's challenging to think about what leadership skills and qualities are needed for the future.

Linking CEO succession to competitive differentiation shifts the conversation from what people personally have time for and want to do, to what they need to make time for, to ensure ongoing relevance in the marketplace. It also sends the message that as an organization, you understand the vital link between sustaining market leadership and developing and nurturing talent over the long term.

Sadly, it's easy for CEOs to pay too little attention to longer-term strategy and succession, focusing instead on the urgent day-to-day challenges of running the business.

Work with the Board to Create a Vision for a Successful CEO Transition

In the same way that you create a vision for your company, it's also prudent to create a vision for a successful CEO transition. Many CEOs miss this step. They forget to apply their strategic visioning capability to the transition itself. Consider: what does a successful CEO transition really look like for you and for the board? Getting alignment on this issue early will create clarity and avoid future challenges as you progress through the transition.

In our view, the best outcome (and our vision of success) is that all stakeholders feel confident that the CEO-elect is the absolute right choice to lead the company into the future, as opposed to the most convenient option. Ideally, having worked closely with the internal candidate for many years, each major stakeholder can attest to the candidate's strategic vision, inspirational leadership to guide the company into the next wave of growth, and ability to continue to win in the marketplace. And you are covered if disaster strikes: you have an emergency candidate who can step in and evoke confidence both within the company and in the marketplace.

This confidence arises as the result of a systematic executive development process that includes clear milestones and accountability, ongoing assessment of potential, exposure to the board, testing culture fit and exhibiting strategic acumen. With this confidence in place you will be more willing to let go and you will feel better about moving on to new (and meaningful) opportunities. This is success!

Organizations who miss this step can find themselves trying to manage misaligned expectations and other challenges. When you have a vision for the transition itself, it will resolve many areas of uncertainty and future frustration.

Develop Leadership Bench Strength

Leadership bench strength has become one measure of a business's future value. Historically, top managers believed they could hire the talent they needed to lead the organization of the future. With changing demographics and shifting attitudes toward taking on risky jobs, this may not be the case today. Top organizations are recognizing that developing internal leaders who are aligned with the company's values pays greater dividends than hiring from the outside. Growing leadership bench strength is not just about training. It's about experiential learning that is aligned with succession planning at all levels in the organization. A strong organization with a solid future has a strong bench of future leaders.

Clarify Roles and Responsibilities

Who does what in the CEO succession process? CEO succession is one of the most important board responsibilities for ensuring business continuity and ongoing value generation, so it's critical to get it right. This can be a place of some confusion and therefore a great opportunity for clarity. In the interviews we conducted, we heard some horror stories about unclear roles between the board chair and CEO. In one case the CEO thought it was her sole responsibility to lead the succession process, so she didn't engage the board every step of the way. The process ended with relationships going sideways when the CEO and the board stepped on each other's toes.

Typically, the board chair leads the succession process for the board by acting as the board's key point of contact. Ideally, the CEO is accountable to create an action plan ensuring different succession scenarios are covered and development plans are in place for a range of candidates. The action plan is usually overseen by the succession committee of the board. Your job as the CEO is to collaborate, develop candidates, manage expectations, communicate with confidence and give valuable input into each candidate's readiness and potential. The head of Human Resources (HR) is typically a key player and advisor on your team.

If the CEO, the board and the succession committee don't collaborate and are not clear about respective roles and accountabilities—and they often are not—it can get messy indeed. Natalie recalls a CEO who called to inquire about help preparing his succession plan. In his mind, he had been grooming his successor for years and the COO was the obvious choice to take over his job. Unfortunately though, the CEO had little buy-in or involvement from the board. When he finally resigned and was keen to appoint his successor, the board stalled. It turns out they wanted to take the company in a new direction and did not want to hire someone in the CEO's likeness. The process unraveled.

In the end, the CEO left with a bad taste in his mouth and a tarnished reputation. The COO quit and the board took a completely different approach to replace the CEO. Sadly, the COO was the one who was hurt by it all. After years of heightened expectations and being told he would get the job, he was left with knocked confidence, a bruised ego and no promotion—a casualty of fuzzy roles and responsibilities in the CEO succession process.

In another situation, one of the CEOs we interviewed recalled an incident where the board chair tried to do it all herself, even trying to force the selection decision alone. As you can imagine, it was not well received as everyone wanted a voice in the process. In this case the board chair took ownership of the process a bit too far.

For many companies the head of HR will act as a resource manager for the CEO and the board succession committee in coordinating and monitoring the process. Often external advisors are engaged to reduce decision biases, provide industry benchmarks and share best practices.

The scenarios above are a good reminder that roles and responsibilities in the succession process need to be crystal clear. When it comes to CEO succession it's not about my way or your way. It's about *our* way—creating a process and approach with all stakeholders that is built on mutual respect, collaboration and a common goal.

Typical CEO Succession Roles
(inspired by the work of Ciampa and Dotlich, 2015)

Board: The board is accountable and responsible for the selection and engagement of the new CEO but must be careful not to compromise the role of the existing CEO. The board should work as a partner with the current CEO.

Board chair: The chair of the board leads the process on behalf of the full board. The chair oversees the appointment of a succession committee and is the key contact for the transition itself, managing communication and negotiations with both the incoming and outgoing CEO. Typically the board chair is a member of the succession committee.

Succession committee: This committee is typically three to six people who thoroughly understand the company's strategy and future business challenges and can translate these into specifications for the next CEO. Often the succession committee includes external members or consultants who can be totally objective and act without decision biases. This committee oversees the internal and external benchmarking of CEO candidates, which includes specifying roles, assessing candidates and mapping possible external candidates.

The committee ensures that key annual milestones are met and, in some cases, it may even get involved in mentoring and developing internal candidates.

CEO: The chief executive officer directs the design and implementation of the transition process. As top internal executive sponsor, the CEO must show commitment to the process. The CEO identifies potential internal successors for the board to consider by linking candidates' development plans to the strategic needs of the business. The CEO mentors and develops potential candidates. As the transition nears, the outgoing CEO sets up the new CEO for success and is willing to step back and let the new person lead.

CHRO: The chief human resources officer helps coordinate the process and advises the current and future CEOs, ensuring that all steps in the succession process are integrated and working. The CHRO makes sure the development of potential talent throughout the organization is planned, structured and formalized. The CHRO helps the CEO create a road map for leadership development options, keeps the process on track and helps manage communication while reporting to the CEO for general leadership development and to the succession committee for CEO succession.

Senior managers on executive committee: The role of the senior leadership team is to prepare the organization for the transition to the new CEO and the inevitable changes this will bring. Regardless of how they themselves may feel about the new CEO, the role of these senior managers is to communicate the "why" behind the transition and to build confidence in the choice. They also support the incoming CEO during the transition and make sure the organization continues to function while adapting to the new leader.

Outside advisors: Often appointed to the succession committee, outside advisors are aware of best practices and can help with key process elements such as candidate identification, external calibration and benchmarking. They can help the committee overcome blind spots and biases that come from working closely with respective candidates in the past.

Managing the Succession Process in Smaller Companies

In smaller companies, the CEO may lead all aspects of the CEO succession process. When this is the case, it is valuable to put an advisory team in place with an external consultant and other trusted advisors to ensure objectivity in candidate identification, selection and development. When CEOs try to manage the process themselves, it can become tarnished by decision biases: CEOs often hire in their likeness rather than based on future needs. Furthermore, decision biases may be created because people tell the CEO what they think the CEO wants to hear rather than the truth about their strategic views and personal needs. This risk can be mitigated somewhat by following a multi-interviewer strategy.

Being Intentional about Leadership

Take Initiative, Don't Avoid It

Human nature draws our attention to the most urgent matters that may threaten our future. For a CEO this shows up as business threats and day-to-day crises. As one CEO of a large, global business commented: "When I became CEO I expected to deal with urgent business matters whenever they arose. What I didn't expect was that urgent matters seemed to occur all the time!" It can feel as if you are fighting fires every day and that your agenda is so full you need to defer anything you can. Unfortunately, your succession may be at the top of the list of items to be deferred. Deferring succession planning is a common pitfall.

Even though CEO selection and the overall succession process are ultimately the board's responsibility, our advice is to get in front of this and view it as an opportunity to show your leadership, to create clarity and confidence, and to build a road map to a place that you desire. When you control the "when" and "how" for initial succession discussions, you will be in a much better proactive leadership position than if you are having to react to the agenda of others.

One CEO cautioned: "The succession discussion can creep up on you and catch you by surprise, especially when things seem to be going well." Taking the initiative will ensure that you are in the right mindset to navigate tricky questions about your life and career goals and allow you to better manage the gush of expectations and rumors rushing toward you. When you are proactive, succession talks will feel more like business and scenario planning than like conversations about pushing you out. If the board instigates the discussion, it can leave you unprepared or feeling vulnerable.

Here is what one CEO had to say about the benefits of a proactive approach:

> The issue was raised every year at the time of my performance review. I talked to the board chair and we had frank discussions about the business and its people, including me. Having this conversation annually made me think more intentionally about my team, the process and my own future. And it made the whole discussion more comfortable; I didn't suspect underground intentions and innuendos. To new CEOs, my advice is don't wait—get ahead of the board on this issue early. It's the board's responsibility to select from the banquet of choices but your responsibility to prepare the menu.

As a point of comparison, here is an example of what can happen when the board chair initiates things unilaterally. As you might expect, it can get very awkward for you. The CEO we spoke with in this case was in the middle of a high-pressure market push when he was approached by the board chair to discuss his succession. He felt blindsided by the conversation and he was suspicious about the chair's intent. Innocent questions from his board chair felt like personal digs:

Do you have a succession plan?
(No, why? Are you planning on firing me?)

How confident are you about the future?
(How confident are you?)

What's your career plan?
(My career plan? I'm just getting going.)

Do you plan on quitting?
(No, do you want me to?)

Looking back, the CEO realized he was sensitive to these questions because they came out of left field and because he found himself unprepared. He now realizes that the chair's inquiry was not about his performance. The board appreciated and valued his contributions; it was simply the board's role to ask these critical questions, and they were doing their job. Faced with a similar situation in the future, he would be the one to instigate succession discussions.

This CEO's comments were echoed by others we spoke with who warned that the first time the "S" word is mentioned, it can feel like the proverbial can of worms is being opened. It's best to be prepared to handle the cascade of logical questions that will be asked of you:

- How long do you plan on staying in this job?
- What do you want to do next?
- Do you have a solid contender on your team now?

- How confident are you in that person's abilities?
- Have you thought about the future company needs in positioning internal candidates?
- We all leave at some point—is it time for a change?

Focus on Others and the Business, Not Your Ego

When the topic of succession comes up, it's important to keep in mind that it's not all about you. That may sound harsh, yet this process will require you to park your ego—and that can be tough for many CEOs. People will be watching you to see how you react as you talk about the future and who may be suited to run the business after you. Will you stay open? Will you encourage healthy discussions without shutting them down? Will you acknowledge your own limitations and development needs? Or will you start to shut down, get overly defensive and react poorly?

When the CEO is egocentric and defensive, problems arise. Such CEOs avoid addressing emotionally charged issues. This is the so-called *soft stuff* that can be so hard. Or they stay so squarely focused on their own interests they lose sight of what is best for the business and for other people.

One of the challenging things about being a CEO is that you must keep taking a hard look at yourself: know your weaknesses and natural inclinations. It's character building for sure. As Socrates is so often quoted as saying: "To know thyself is the beginning of wisdom." In our experience, as former executives and now executive coaches, this wisdom only comes over time and through experience. It is not revealed in a leadership assessment. Indeed, you must live the CEO job to really know yourself as a leader—how you handle opportunities and challenges that come your way.

Yet as ripe as the CEO role is for growth, it's just as easy to get caught up in the image and power of the day job and to come to believe that your needs matter the most, especially when so many people are catering to them. You need to recognize that they are catering to the job you have, not to you as a person. We can't stress enough how important it is to shake off the trappings of power and ego during succession planning.

Through our research, we found that the CEOs who were most effective had a mindset squarely centered on the business and other people. They expressed genuine satisfaction in seeing the company succeed beyond their tenure. They cared about their executive team and wanted them to succeed in their careers. Paradoxically, they stayed focused on others as one way to manage their own negative emotions when they arose.

Communication in Critical Moments

Craft Your Compelling Why and Share It with Others

In the early stages of succession planning, your primary communication task is to communicate your compelling *why* for the process: Why does succession matter to you and the business you lead? Why are you doing this? Why now? Forget comments like "We are engaging in succession planning so we are protected if someone is hit by a bus or wins the lotto," implying that as soon as someone gets a cash windfall they are out of there! You will want to create your own narrative that is much more authentic and inspiring.

We recommend you articulate an inspirational message that gets people excited about what you are trying to achieve. An inspirational message is like a marketing tool: it shapes the whole experience. A marketing and digital agency we spoke with was masterful with this concept, no surprise given that their expertise is connecting with people. When asked about their "why" for succession, they said: "It can be summed up in two words: we believe."

One of the partners said:

CEO succession is another sign that *we believe* in the future of the company; *we believe* in our executive team's potential to take us there; and, ultimately, *we believe* in the potential of each person on the team.

In our view, this is the gold standard for a compelling rationale for CEO succession planning. It tells key stakeholders that the process is not solely focused on the business's needs. Rather, each stakeholder matters and has the potential for a compelling career and future. It also taps into people's aspirations. It causes people to pause and think: *Do they believe in me? Do I believe in this company?*

When crafting your compelling why for succession, be aware that the board often views succession primarily through a risk-management lens. You will want to ensure that you satisfy their need for risk management, but don't let them hijack your messaging. You will want to come up with something more progressive for your different audiences and true to your organizational culture.

Adding to this, many organizations frame their communication about succession planning as a much broader talent management program that looks at development needs at all levels. In this context, a publication by Smith, Wellins and Paese of Development Dimensions International defines talent management as "the recruitment, development, promotion and retention of people, planned and executed in line with the organization's current and future business goals." This approach shifts the mindset on CEO succession from emergency replacement to longer-term talent and leadership development which creates value for the business today and is more meaningful for its culture.

Keep in mind, if you have lackluster talent management and cultural practices, then you may breed cynicism if you are too aspirational with your why. To avoid this, be clear that this process is the first step in a broader intent to focus on people, and then keep coming back to it. Key stakeholders will need to hear your why a few times to really believe it.

☒ Political Pitfalls

Fooling Yourself that a List of Names on a Spreadsheet Is Enough

Some CEOs believe that they have a CEO succession plan when they have a list of CEO candidates' names on a spreadsheet that they can present to their board. Don't fall into this trap! One experienced former CEO shared a retrospective view:

> Having a list of names is at least a starting point, yet it is by no means a confidence builder and [it] lacks

credibility. It's like writing down your views on strategy and telling others to adopt it. Good luck with that.

CEO transitions pose extraordinary risk for companies and their enterprise value. Having a vision for your CEO transition and following the six-phase process in this book will increase your probability of success and reduce your risk.

✓ In Summary

Start early in your mandate to work with the board to reduce the emotional charge of succession planning. Taking initiative and leading the succession discussion will reduce the inevitable emotional charge. Don't get caught unprepared. Approaching succession planning like an investor can add value to the business. Build a credible succession road map by thinking long-term, beyond your current mandate as CEO, and planning for that future. Link succession planning to the business strategy to defuse emotions. Focus on the needs of the business and the needs of the candidates, in addition to considering the implications for yourself. Create clarity up front on the key roles and accountabilities of all stakeholders in the succession process (CEO, board chair, succession committee, CHRO, senior managers and outside advisors). There is no magic bullet for CEO succession that applies to all companies. Adapt the process to your own situation, company culture and strategy. Envision the company's future and your compelling "why" for being proactive in succession so you can communicate with confidence, courage and clarity.

Getting started on any task that is non-routine can be hard, especially when it is not part of your day-to-day imperatives. We hope the approaches that successful CEOs have used to get going, plus the commentary in this chapter, have provided you with a few ideas for making succession a rewarding experience.

As CEO, you have many responsibilities which can be delegated and supported by others. Yet for your succession you must be courageous and confident as the solitary leader. Yes, it is lonely at the top, especially for your own succession! You want to create the future by being proactive, not let it develop in unexpected ways. Here are some self-coaching questions to get you started on your succession leadership journey.

⟨?⟩ Self-Coaching Questions

- What is holding you back from starting the CEO succession process?

- Are you clear on who you need to be as a CEO to lead an effective succession? What leadership qualities are important for you?

- Have you aligned the overall succession process with the business's future needs and linked it to your strategic plans?

- If succession is not happening in your business, might it be that you are part of the problem?

- How adaptive is your organization?

- What is your compelling reason for doing this? Is it a reason beyond risk management?

- What key principles/values do you want to model to your team and board as you engage in the process?

2

BE PROACTIVE: BENCHMARK THE ROLE

Key Leadership Quality

Be proactive. Benchmark the role. Make things happen rather than react when a potential problem hits. Self-manage in awkward moments.

When we began discussing the success profile of the future CEO, it felt like the board was communicating directly to me about the things they felt I was not doing well. Initially this upset me because the board had not mentioned any of these things in my performance review. Then it hit me: they were not talking about me! They were talking about what was needed in a future CEO.

THE RIGHT CEO can make your company millions of dollars—and the wrong CEO can cost you millions, perhaps even the company! It's worth the effort to slow down and figure out the qualities you need in the future CEO so you can increase your odds of finding the right fit.

It can be tempting to skip over this process (or give it minimal attention) by convincing yourself that you (and the board) have made many senior hires in the past and this is just another; it's nothing to get too excited about. This is one of the common mistakes you will want to avoid. Instead, create a CEO success profile—an overview of the skills and attributes needed in a future CEO. It's critical for bench-marking candidates and setting expectations. It's a small part of the process that is actually a big part of success. If you skip it, you risk creating blind spots, bottlenecks and politics down the road.

To get you started, we share a sample profile, a gold mine of information on what distinguishes world-class CEOs. Our suggestion is that you and the board spend time really thinking about this profile and which elements are going to be instrumental for your competitive differentiation down the road.

What Successful CEOs Do

Understand What Differentiates Top-Performing CEOs

Think of the CEO success profile that follows as a buffet of information you get to choose from. Here's why. It includes twelve criteria (in bold below) that distinguish top-performing CEOs. To create it, we reviewed North American awards that recognize the best CEOs and companies. By using this profile as a starting point you can be confident that you're comparing your future CEO candidates to the criteria used for champions in the field.

We reviewed the following awards: *Fortune*'s Most Admired Company, Deloitte's Best Managed Company, Ernst & Young's Entrepreneur of the Year, Canada's Outstanding CEO of the Year, ChiefExecutive.net's CEO of the Year and *Fortune*'s Businessperson of the Year.

Sample CEO Success Profile

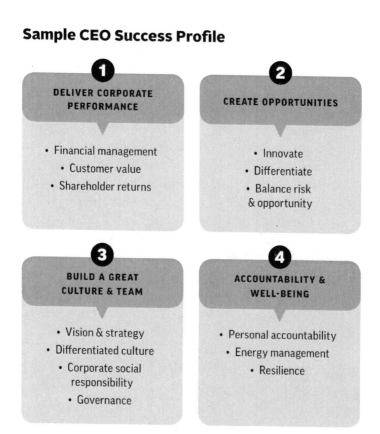

1 DELIVER CORPORATE PERFORMANCE

- Financial management
- Customer value
- Shareholder returns

2 CREATE OPPORTUNITIES

- Innovate
- Differentiate
- Balance risk & opportunity

3 BUILD A GREAT CULTURE & TEAM

- Vision & strategy
- Differentiated culture
- Corporate social responsibility
- Governance

4 ACCOUNTABILITY & WELL-BEING

- Personal accountability
- Energy management
- Resilience

Sample CEO Success Profile Details

1. Deliver Corporate Performance

- **Financial management:** Deliver top-line financial metrics.
- **Customer value:** Perform on key customer metrics relative to industry benchmarks.

- **Shareholder returns:** Build company value that leads to shareholder returns; make appropriate trade-offs between the short and the long term.

2. Create Opportunities

- **Innovate:** Drive company success by pioneering innovative approaches and investing in new initiatives; manage initiatives to ensure return on investment.
- **Differentiate:** Boost competitiveness by defining the company's products/services and seizing opportunities that differentiate the company and lead to growth (mergers/acquisitions, aligned business models, new markets/services, etc.); deliver excellent results relative to competitors.
- **Balance risk & opportunity:** Balance opportunity-seeking and risk management when making decisions about the business.

3. Build a Great Culture & Team

- **Vision & strategy:** Craft a vision and strategy that inspire new levels of personal engagement, revenue growth, career growth, achievement and industry recognition; create alignment across teams and geographies.
- **Differentiated culture:** Create a culture that differentiates the company and demonstrate how that culture improves results, engagement and team capabilities; proactively grow and develop people, build teams and develop succession candidates.
- **Corporate social responsibility:** Lead corporate social responsibility initiatives; role model commitment to

social and environmental stewardship and community engagement.

- **Governance:** Clarify governance roles and engage with stakeholders; set appropriate boundaries between board oversight and management responsibilities for day-to-day operations; collaborate with the board chair to ensure effective oversight of corporate governance, risk management and reporting.

4. Accountability & Well-Being

- **Personal accountability:** Model personal accountability and assertively deliver results.
- **Energy management:** Manage personal well-being and energy.
- **Resilience:** Demonstrate personal resilience and a non-anxious presence in times of pressure and stress.

Find Your Pivot Points

To use this profile effectively, hone in on the attributes that are critically important for your business success. Ram Charan, a management guru and best-selling author, recommended in a recent *Harvard Business Review* article that you and the board focus on your *pivot points,* a short list of a few critical skills and attributes that will make or break the future CEO and the company. Take a look at the profile to determine which factors will be the most important for driving growth and sustainable success in your business; debate this with the board until you have full agreement on your pivot points.

Here is how one CEO we interviewed used the profile in his business. Mark, as we'll call him, runs a large manufacturing company that services North American customers. His industry is challenged by hyper-competition and by lower-cost competitors. Mark and his board identified three pivot points which they believed were key for driving growth and positioning the company for the future: (1) product development, (2) knowledge of technical advancements and (3) experience creating a consistent customer experience in a geographically dispersed company. Take note: Mark was a not a technology guy. Identifying technology as a pivot point made him uncomfortable. It was clear to everyone involved in the conversation that he was lacking one of the key qualities needed for the future, a common dynamic we will discuss later in this chapter.

It's worth highlighting that the pivot point approach is the exact opposite of the "Chief of Everything" description often used for the CEO job, a phrase made famous by Peter Drucker, perhaps one of the most famous business writers of all time. Although "Chief of Everything" may be the reality of a CEO's job, this description is not helpful when it comes to qualifying candidates or pinpointing development needs. We advocate getting more specific. Consider: what will really drive your strategy and make a difference to your future success?

Adapt Culture to Improve Performance

One of the trickiest parts of a CEO success profile is clarifying what "culture fit" means (a make-or-break factor for CEOs). In our view, there are two valuable questions to ask here: (1) What are the elements of your current company culture that you want to preserve? and (2) What elements do you want to enhance or change? In order to be strategic about "culture fit," you will want to identify the main attributes of your culture and what cultural elements enable or inhibit company performance so that you can magnify some qualities and downplay others.

A very interesting study by Chad Hartnell published in the *Journal of Applied Psychology* found that when hiring a CEO, it's more important to consider how the new CEO will complement what exists in the culture today than to hire for sameness. This means you don't necessarily hire a future CEO in your "cultural likeness." You hire for complementary differences.

For example, if the current CEO is highly task-oriented, but high-touch customer relationships are a key part of the future strategy, the company may benefit from someone who is more relationship-oriented and focused on communication, coordination of efforts and encouragement of participation. If the current CEO is highly relationship-focused to the point that it's an overused strength in the culture, then the company may benefit from a more task-oriented person as CEO. This study proposes that hiring complementary qualities, rather than the same qualities, leads to an improvement in performance.

Following this same line of thinking, the Conference Board and RW2 Industries, along with Development Dimensions International, partnered with fourteen US organizations to understand better what millennial leaders believe is important to prepare them for future C-suite roles. A 2017 article by Jon Spector and Ron Williams in *Fortune* pointed out that what current CEOs see as important attributes for up-and-coming CEO candidates is different from what millennials view as important. For millennial leaders, some of the most important attributes are CEOs with strong interpersonal skills, emotional intelligence and communication skills. By contrast, what tops the list for today's CEOs are critical-thinking skills, business know-how and an ability to managestakeholders. The key here is that both points of view need to be considered; they are both important for the jigsaw puzzle of "fit." CEOs can't just groom candidates in their likeness. When thinking about the future CEO, they will want to break old patterns, rethink standard frameworks and start talking about how the role needs to evolve.

Of course, not all differences between leadership and culture are going to be positive. We have all experienced a dreaded hire who is like a bull in a china shop, finding opportunities to criticize at every turn or disrespecting all the great work from the past. From our experience, these don't typically work out. Time and energy wasted, more grief for all. As you will discover in Chapter 5, no matter how different the new CEO is, he or she will need to strike a delicate balance—bring a fresh approach to the role while honoring the past, and be respectful and thoughtful above all else.

What Kind of CEO Drives Financial Results?

One revealing study, conducted in 2008 by Geoff Smart and Randy Street, stood out for us during our review of research on the link between CEO success profiles and CEO performance.

To learn whether there is a profile that can predict CEO success, the authors teamed up with Steven Kaplan, a professor of entrepreneurship and finance at the University of Chicago, and his collaborators, Morten Sorensen and Mark Klebanov. Together they analyzed data from 313 topgrading interviews they had conducted on private-equity-backed CEOs from 2000 to 2005. (Topgrading is known as one of the most effective and validated interview methods available. In the methodology, candidates undergo a twelve-step process that includes extensive interviews, a score card, research into job history, identification of career patterns and extensive reference checking.) Then the researchers matched the CEOs' assessments with the actual financial performance they delivered.

What they found is that emotional intelligence is important, but only when combined with the propensity to get things done. The CEOs who delivered the best financial performance had soft skills (and soft skills were an important part of their ascent to the top), but they also knew when to stop collaborating and to focus proactively on achieving key outcomes that moved the company forward.

Based on this research, when looking for someone with CEO potential, look for a candidate who is adept at balancing soft skills and the need to collaborate with the ability to act decisively when it is necessary to be quick and results-focused.

 # Being Intentional about Leadership

Self-Manage in Awkward Moments

As you can imagine, all this talk about what is needed in a future CEO can be uncomfortable for the current leader. One CEO we spoke with was refreshingly candid about what discussions were like for him personally:

> When you first start talking about what is needed in a future CEO, it can feel like a discussion about your own inadequacies. You wonder: would I even make the cut if they were doing the search today? It feels awkward!

He went further and shared how he dealt with his discomfort:

> After our first discussion on this topic, I was tempted to avoid the discussions altogether. Then I asked myself: What are the expectations I have of myself in this situation? Am I living up to my own expectations for a great CEO? In the end, I concluded that being a great CEO means having a clear vision and strategy for the future and seeing it through. In this case, it meant a vision for the *next* CEO.

It's helpful to be prepared for this discomfort and not get blindsided by it. A heads-up: it *really* can be uncomfortable!

Clearly, managing through these potentially uncomfortable conversations will be an important aspect of your legacy as CEO. Fortunately, there is one thing you can do here that will have a big positive impact: set the agenda for this discussion rather than reacting to the requests of others. Any board worth their weight will surely raise this issue, so you may as well take the plunge and proactively ask: What capabilities do we need in a future CEO if we want this business to thrive? How do we need the next CEO to be different from me?

Communication in Critical Moments

Go Beyond Benchmarking Candidates: Start Career Conversations

Beyond talking about the business requirements, the CEO success profile is an effective tool for career conversations with candidates. Fundamentally, it's a communication tool.

It is valuable to ask CEO candidates to benchmark themselves against the profile and the criteria for top-performing CEOs. This will allow them to assess their current strengths and gaps and to pinpoint their growth areas. It also generates a conversation about the complexity of the role and the fact that it can be lonely at the top because of the job's relentless demands.

If you want to model a true "learning spirit," consider benchmarking yourself using the criteria as well and then compare and contrast your scores to future CEO contenders. This will certainly spark an interesting conversation about the journey to CEO and what it takes to prepare candidates for the job. And you may even come up with some fresh development goals for yourself along the way.

Use Your CEO Success Profile to Benchmark Candidates

Ask candidates to rate themselves (on a scale of 1 to 5) to identify their strengths and to pinpoint any development needs.

1. DELIVER CORPORATE PERFORMANCE	VERY DISSATISFIED	DISSATISFIED	NEUTRAL	SATISFIED	VERY SATISFIED
Financial	1	2	3	4	5
Customer value	1	2	3	4	5
Shareholder returns	1	2	3	4	5

2. CREATE OPPORTUNITIES					
Innovate	1	2	3	4	5
Differentiate	1	2	3	4	5
Balance risk and opportunity	1	2	3	4	5

3. BUILD A GREAT CULTURE & TEAM					
Vision & strategy	1	2	3	4	5
Differentiated culture	1	2	3	4	5
Corporate social responsibility	1	2	3	4	5
Governance	1	2	3	4	5

4. ACCOUNTABILITY & WELL-BEING					
Personal accountability	1	2	3	4	5
Energy management	1	2	3	4	5
Resilience	1	2	3	4	5

✖ Political Pitfalls

Ignoring Doubts and Insecurities

As you go through this phase, be aware that insecurity may be rampant. Let's be honest here. The board is insecure because you have such an important job and they rely on your passion and energy to succeed. For them, managing you is like a coach managing a star athlete. They might worry that if they push you (the star player) too hard on future matters, they risk throwing you off your game, or worse, losing you to another team. It's nerve-racking for them to approach you about succession, especially when you are playing to win right now. What if you leave? What if you get distracted and performance goes down? What if things get political?

If executives get wind of a CEO succession discussion, they can become insecure too. Will they lose their favorite boss? Get a new boss they won't like? If they put their hat in the ring for the CEO job, will someone call them on their bluff and reveal their weaknesses, implying they don't have what it takes to progress? Worse yet, will their colleague get the job? "Oh no, I don't want to report to *that* so-and-so." As soon as succession gets talked about, a can of worms gets opened.

And, of course (dare we say it), you might be insecure too. You may worry about the consequences of not having a successor or that a successor won't be ready on time. Let's face it, you may worry about being pushed out, about sending the message you are thinking of moving on, about whether you have what it takes to lead the company into the future—the list goes on and on.

We believe that one sure way to deal with this insecurity is to be intentional about your leadership and have a well-considered process. When you are intentional about stepping up and proactively leading—meaning that you set a vision, communicate clearly and stand firmly on the importance of trust and relationships—anxiety starts to melt. The stakeholders can breathe a sigh of relief and get to work on the game plan. Of course, if they know the game plan, all the better.

 **In Summary**

Throughout this chapter we have shared some process tips and tools that hopefully will get you started on the development of a CEO success profile. We also highlighted opportunities for you to manage your emotions, live your values and lead with conviction—aspects of being a successful CEO. To support you further along this phase of the journey we offer the following self-coaching questions.

 Self-Coaching Questions

- What actions might you take to improve your working relationship with the board so you can lead the initiative of creating a CEO success profile that aligns with future strategic goals?

- Have you created the context for discussing future CEO success profiles with the board and your team as a developmental journey?

- How do you plan to ensure alignment of your CEO success profile with key stakeholders?

- When you benchmark yourself with the generic attributes of CEO success, what skills and capabilities, including ones you don't have, will help drive future growth?

- What pivotal skills and attributes do you foresee as distinguishing the next CEO?

- What has your executive development journey been as a CEO? What part of your story would you like to share with CEO candidates to help them prepare?

3

BE CURIOUS: IDENTIFY CANDIDATES

Key Leadership Quality

Be curious. Identify candidates. Ask questions of candidates with the intent to really learn about them. Give them your full attention as you listen to their answers.

I worked with a team for years and believed that they all wanted my job as CEO—who wouldn't want the top job? When I asked my top candidate, she said she wasn't interested. I learned then that I should have listened more carefully and not made assumptions.

OPEN AND candid career conversations are at the core of candidate identification. As one CEO advises: "Don't take career conversations lightly. These conversations likely mean more to the candidates than to you. They will certainly be dinner conversation for the candidate." We couldn't agree more.

In this chapter, we outline the different succession scenarios you will need to anticipate. We give you a framework for having meaningful (not superficial) career conversations, an approach we created using research on what defines CEO potential. Another important takeaway is a template for reporting to the board on your CEO succession pipeline.

However, with this phase, it's important not to get too caught up in the framework and tools. What really counts is how you show up in the conversations. Are you building trust? Are you focused on relationships? Are you open and curious about others?

Who has the potential to be the next CEO?

CEO Candidate Identification—Process Elements and Toolkit

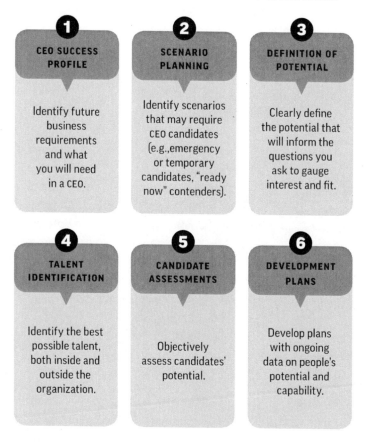

1 CEO SUCCESS PROFILE

Identify future business requirements and what you will need in a CEO.

2 SCENARIO PLANNING

Identify scenarios that may require CEO candidates (e.g.,emergency or temporary candidates, "ready now" contenders).

3 DEFINITION OF POTENTIAL

Clearly define the potential that will inform the questions you ask to gauge interest and fit.

4 TALENT IDENTIFICATION

Identify the best possible talent, both inside and outside the organization.

5 CANDIDATE ASSESSMENTS

Objectively assess candidates' potential.

6 DEVELOPMENT PLANS

Develop plans with ongoing data on people's potential and capability.

What Successful CEOs Do

Focus on Building Trust and Having High-Quality Conversations

We find that many currently published resources on CEO succession fail to highlight adequately how vital it is to build trust and manage emotions during the entire succession process.

Historically, CEOs have been encouraged to leave emotions out of business, especially when interacting with their direct reports. Thankfully those days are behind us. We encourage you, during the candidate identification process, to become more aware of emotions—both your own and the candidate's—and to be curious about how the candidates, given their stage in life, feel about becoming a CEO. This personal insight will complement a more objective evaluation later of how candidates measure up on key criteria.

If you take this approach, it is likely your CEO candidates will notice and value your efforts. To put this in perspective, here is a comment from one up-and-coming CEO we interviewed:

> I really wish that somebody had a deeper conversation with me centered on my desire for the role and what I

perceived as my strengths and weaknesses. They should have addressed the potential challenges I would encounter, and where I saw the opportunity for me and my family. We touched on this issue lightly yet, to me, it felt like a gap in the process.

From a different vantage point, learn from one CEO who has been down this road before and shares some regrets over the way he approached the process:

As I look back... the whole process would have been easier if we had better, and different, conversations. I wish I spent more time talking about the human stuff—asking better questions and describing what the transition to CEO was like for me personally so that others could learn from it and decide if they really wanted the job.

Why are trust and thoughtful conversations so important? In our view, it's because of the uncertainty that comes with CEO succession. No matter how much succession planning you do, you don't know how it will turn out or exactly how it will unfold. You can hope and anticipate it will work out well, but there is risk involved. For it to turn out well, the conditions must be right. Setting expectations is also important—it's possible the mutual investment may not yield anything tangible, or one of you may lose the investment entirely.

Because of this uncertainty and by their very nature, succession conversations can elicit either openness and connection or judgment and fear. Trust and the quality of the relationship are what enable you to work through this: to learn what others need and want, to understand what they have to offer and to share what you need as well. It's the starting point for crafting opportunities that benefit mutual interests and prepare the candidate for navigating the future.

Be warned though: you might think you have trust while others see it differently. Natalie once worked with a CEO in the venture capital industry who was certain three executives on his team wanted the CEO role and he had a robust succession plan. This was not the case. When Natalie interviewed each of the executives about their respective career goals, it was clear that none of them wanted the job. They'd just given up telling the CEO because every time they tried he said, "You will want it when you get it." Even though this CEO had confidence in his succession plan and the board was convinced he had managed succession risk, his plan wasn't worth the paper it was written on. Without trust, there is more uncertainty, not less.

Put simply: if you pay attention to trust and are curious about how people feel and what they want, you will perform better here. We advise you to put yourself in the candidate's shoes and imagine you are watching yourself on video when having these conversations. What would you see? Do your emotional state and candor demonstrate that you are genuinely interested in the candidate?

Approaching these conversations in a genuine and open manner will help you avoid political games—a situation where candidates tell you one thing but mean something else. This will give you more confidence in your succession data. After all, a candidate's motives and aspirations are a critical piece of the information you use for making decisions about who you want to invest in and where to put your time and energy.

When CEOs place too much emphasis on outcome goals, personal credentials and scenario plans, or they avoid career conversations altogether, this can lead to a vicious cycle resulting in failure. It discounts the importance of the human element in CEO succession.

Plan for Different Succession Scenarios

As well as trust and effective communication, scenario planning is another practical way to navigate an uncertain future. There are at least three scenarios you'll want to make sure you cover off in your CEO succession plan, meaning you identify candidates for each scenario. In an ideal world, you create multiple candidate options for each scenario, instead of relying on just one.

Scenario A: The Emergency Candidate

An emergency CEO candidate is someone who can step in temporarily—the replacement scenario—if anything happens to you such as an illness, a family emergency or even a sudden resignation. An emergency candidate typically comes from your sphere of influence—an executive on your team who has earned your confidence and that of the board, a board member or a consultant. The emergency candidate is a stopgap while an expedited search is conducted by the board. Ideally announced within twenty-four hours of the emergency, the appointment conveys a sense of order and control to the market and employees. In an ideal world, one or more emergency candidates are known to the board at all times and this list is updated regularly, typically annually.

Scenario B: The "Ready Now" Candidate

This is the ideal succession scenario. In the succession plan there are three or more people identified that both you and the board believe can take over the top job *and* they want the role. Over the years you have positioned these candidates for the job and they have sufficient business and operational exposure to hit the ground running. When the time comes, the heavy lifting has been done and you're simply working through the selection process with the board taking the lead. Ironically, if you have done this well, you will experience pain. In this case, it's not the pain of being without someone; it's the pain of choosing between several good candidates!

Most companies don't have three "ready now" candidates so they categorize their top people according to their degree of readiness: ready now, ready in one to two years, ready in three to five years and so on, with gaps and risks highlighted for each person.

When the CEO role becomes available, the company can weigh the potential risks of hiring each candidate as well as the probability of success. If you have a strong executive team that can pull their weight, you may get by with hiring a

CEO candidate who shows potential but has less experience. It's less risky when the team is strong.

When evaluating a candidate's readiness, it's important to distinguish between current performance and the ability to progress to the next level of taking on different and more complex responsibilities. For internal candidates it can be tempting to rely heavily on past performance data. We heard in our interviews comments like: "We knew the candidate well because he has been in the organization for years and we have watched him progress." While this is an important piece of the puzzle, don't fall into the trap of relying on past performance. Past performance is the best predictor of future performance—but only in similar conditions and circumstances.

When considering the next CEO, you will want to adopt a future performance mindset that focuses on what could be, rather than entirely on what has happened. This shift in mindset goes hand in hand with a curiosity mindset, prompting you to focus on vision, future market opportunities and the candidate's strengths. At this point it can be helpful to cycle back to Phase 1 of the succession process when you worked with the board and others to create a vision of the company in the future and what kind of leadership will be required. When evaluating readiness, it can be helpful to answer the question: Ready for what?

Scenario C: The External Possibilities

Most companies look externally and internally when a CEO vacancy becomes available, so coming up with some external candidates early makes practical sense and it gives the board comfort that you have done your due diligence. Alternatively, if you don't think you will have a successor internally or they won't be ready on time, consider identifying external candidates as a third possible scenario.

Quick side note: if you put external candidates on your CEO succession list, make sure you guard it with your life. One company included external candidates on their list, with the addition of private details from career conversations they had with the candidates they knew well. Mysteriously, the list got distributed to a few managers. Lo and behold, the next day one of the managers saw an external candidate at a hockey game and said: "So, I hear you don't like your job." You can only imagine what happened next.

Define Potential in Specific Terms

Keeping these scenarios in mind, you will want to talk to each candidate about their respective career goals. To do this, we offer another tool in your CEO succession toolkit: a model of CEO potential. The model goes beyond the job specifications; it also includes elements such as personal motivation and career aspirations, two important considerations for fit.

We built the model based on the Corporate Executive Board's research on drivers of potential and on Hogan Assessments' research on what leads to executive success or derails it. The model includes four components that need to be explored with each person before you can determine whether the candidate truly has the potential to be a successful CEO.

Model of potential

(adapted from CEB High-Potential Solution)

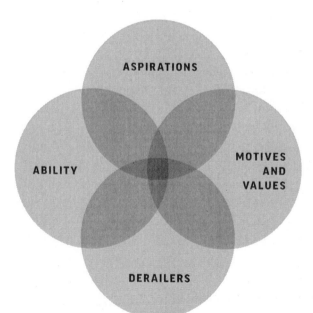

The High-Potential Model

1. **Aspirations.** Ideally you're seeking candidates who want the CEO job and whose life and career plans fit with the demands of the role. The more their personal aspirations align with the CEO role, the higher their potential, as they will likely put in the discretionary effort needed to succeed.

2. **Ability.** This component refers to the degree to which candidates meet the specifications in your CEO success profile. It can also refer to cognitive ability, emotional intelligence, personal strengths and behavioral tendencies—all well-established predictors of CEO performance. The higher the ability, the higher your chance of success.

3. **Motives and Values.** The first question you will likely ask CEO candidates is: Do you want this job? In our view, more important questions are: (1) *Why* do you want this job? and (2) Do you understand what the CEO job is all about? Each candidate's motivations really matter. What are the parts of the CEO job that align with what is important to them? What are the parts that may be at odds with what they believe is important?

Individuals who value challenges tend to take on more responsibility and thrive in the CEO role. Also, when people are motivated to do the CEO job for intrinsic reasons (challenge, meaning, service) as opposed to extrinsic ones (money, power, recognition), it's a sign of fit. A key part of assessing potential is understanding what motivates people and what they value as human beings. It's important to check for alignment between people's motives and the requirements of the role.

4. Derailers. When people are challenged or under great stress, their behavioral tendencies tend to be exposed—both the good ones and the bad ones. Put someone in a CEO job with tough market conditions and political naysayers, and the conditions are ripe! Although people's bad behavioral tendencies in such situations—their derailers—may be a result of weaknesses, they can also stem from their overused strengths. As part of your due diligence, you'll want to consider what might derail each CEO candidate and be attuned to common derailers.

According to a 2012 article from Hogan Assessment Systems, "CEOs Aren't Like Us," by Hogan partner David Winsborough, there are two common CEO derailers. The first is what Winsborough calls the tendency to be mischievous: to dominate others through charm, impulsivity and nonconformist behavior. Although CEOs with this tendency are exciting to work with at their best; at their worst they may dominate others, can be poor at managing time and may cut corners.

The second common derailer is the tendency to be colorful: to be gregarious, flirtatious and to see themselves at center stage. These CEOs tend to be socially dominant and action-oriented at their best; at their worst they can be forceful, pushy and egocentric.

Other derailers that Winsborough describes include the tendency for some CEOs to over-rely on what worked for them in the past rather than pay attention to the current situation and context. They tend to be ruthless about cutting out people who are not 100 percent behind them, and they can be oblivious to social and political contexts.

Because derailers can distract CEO candidates from ever reaching their potential, they can make the board's life difficult after promotion. We recommend that the board consider whether the candidate is aware of what might derail them and explore whether the candidate has coping strategies in place for managing derailers should they pop up. The board may also want to consider organizational derailers: what is happening in the organization which may get in the way of developing each person.

Tip: How to Uncover Derailers

Hogan Assessments has a psychometric report that highlights candidate derailers. Another simple method is to put candidates through an opinion-based derailer test—simply ask the hiring committee to write down five things that they believe might derail the candidate and then assign a probability that it will occur. If it's a high-probability derailer, you can put a risk-management plan in place, or think twice about your choice of candidate.

Identify and Validate Your Succession Picks

In most of the companies we approached, there is a planned and somewhat structured formal process for identifying CEO candidates. Typically the CEO identifies internal contenders, paying attention to the CEO success profile and the four components of the high-potential model just discussed. Then the succession committee of the board meets to review the pool and weigh in. It's a team effort, and the process will likely go sideways if any one stakeholder takes too much ownership of it.

Once initial candidates have been identified, a more rigorous process takes place for validating each candidate's strengths and development areas. This usually includes group discussions to ensure consideration of different points of view as well as reviews of more objective data, such as leadership 360s, engagement ratings, leadership assessments and reviews of past accomplishments. Some companies use a simple nine-box performance and assessment matrix to guide discussions about candidates. If you do an Internet search for "nine-box matrix," you'll find many examples of this popular tool online.

Finally, many companies consider the best predictor of potential is how a candidate performs when given increasingly complex job assignments that align with the business strategy and reflect the type of work that a CEO is responsible for. We offer suggestions about developmental assignments in Chapter 4, so for now it's sufficient to say that, as time goes on, candidates stay on the high-potential list based on how well they achieve these increasingly challenging performance goals.

One CEO we spoke with shared how this works in his company, a large and well-established family-owned business. He identified the future CEO using an enterprise-wide strategy, framed as a larger cultural initiative that emphasized the value of talent development across multiple levels of leadership. The board's succession committee created a database of fifty people in the company who had the potential to progress in the business (similar to the succession management process advocated by James Peters of Korn Ferry on page 84). Each person went through a career exploration exercise to clarify their personal vision; then a leadership assessment tool was used to identify their strengths and gaps. As a result, each person received a development plan. To drive accountability to complete their respective plans, each person was held accountable to share their progress at regular intervals not only with their manager but also with their teammates. This company-wide approach helped to scale executive development throughout the firm and created a pool of key people prepared to take on more. They felt comfortable that the future CEO would be identified from this roster of candidates and that the candidates' performance would be enhanced by the process.

Below is a sample report you can use to track your efforts and report progress to the board.

Talent Identification Report

(adapted from CEB High-Potential Solution)

CEO SUCCESSION PLAN

POSITION TITLE	CEO
SUCCESSION CANDIDATE	Joe Smith
INTERNAL OR EXTERNAL	Internal
READINESS RANKING	1
RETENTION RISK	Med
CAREER GOALS	Interested in role
DEVELOPMENT ACTION	Moving into COO role to gain experience running multi-functional operations.
WHY IMPORTANT	All experience to date is running operational area where has direct functional expertise. Has not led cross-functional executives.
WHAT SUCCESS LOOKS LIKE	Delivery on business outcomes for one-year assignment and positive leadership 360 with executive team.
POTENTIAL DERAILERS	Retention risk; stress; and letting go of control.
RISK PLAN	Put in place retention plan with CEO. Hire executive coach to work on letting go.

READINESS RANKING
1 – Ready in one year. Essentially ready now. **2** – Ready in two to three years.
3 – Ready in three to five years. **Emergency** – Could temporarily fulfill role.

POSITION TITLE	CEO
SUCCESSION CANDIDATE	Bob Callers
INTERNAL OR EXTERNAL	Internal
READINESS RANKING	Emergency
RETENTION RISK	Low
CAREER GOALS	Not interested in role permanently due to balance implications
DEVELOPMENT ACTION	Ensure has relationships with board members.
WHY IMPORTANT	Want to ensure has credibility and relationships with board.
WHAT SUCCESS LOOKS LIKE	Board chair and board express high level of comfort with candidate.
POTENTIAL DERAILERS	If position vacant too long and personal sacrifice extends beyond six months, could lead to retention issue.
RISK PLAN	If emergency unfolds, put in place retention bonus. Ensure search is expedited.

POSITION TITLE	CEO
SUCCESSION CANDIDATE	Cindy Freeman
INTERNAL OR EXTERNAL	External
READINESS RANKING	1
RETENTION RISK	Low
CAREER GOALS	Currently CEO with competitor but has expressed interest in role with broader scope.
DEVELOPMENT ACTION	
WHY IMPORTANT	
WHAT SUCCESS LOOKS LIKE	Delivery on business outcomes for one-year assignment and positive leadership 360 with executive team.
POTENTIAL DERAILERS	May not be available when role available.
RISK PLAN	Board member to stay in contact and touch base for informal annual meeting.

READINESS RANKING

1 – Ready in one year. Essentially ready now. **2** – Ready in two to three years.
3 – Ready in three to five years. **Emergency** – Could temporarily fulfill role.

The Seven CEOs

In his publication *The Seven CEOs*, James Peters advocates that succession planning is more than having one person to take over the CEO role. A deeper talent pipeline is needed. Peters puts forward the idea that an organization needs seven CEO candidates—the current senior leader plus six others at various stages in their career development. To achieve such robust succession management, every organization needs to consider: who are your seven CEOs and what should you do to prepare them? This approach requires a more holistic view of succession, one that views it as an ongoing process that extends throughout the organization. We would add that it is valuable to consider the diversity within your CEO pipeline to ensure there is both gender and cultural diversity.

Do Formal Leadership Assessments

Another way to validate initial candidate picks is to use leadership assessments (there are many available assessment tools in common usage). We chuckled when one CEO gave us his rationale for formal assessments: "Assessing your CEO candidates is like assessing your children. After years of working with them, it's hard to be objective."

When it comes time to assess CEO candidates formally, most organizations use an outsourced process. Organizational psychologists use a full complement of assessments to evaluate a leader's style, behavioral tendencies, cognitive abilities and problem-solving skills. CEO assessments typically involve psychometrics, in-depth interviews and strategic-thinking simulations. The best assessments also compare candidates against other CEOs or industry leaders. Although not a single CEO we spoke to reported having a major epiphany from the use of leadership assessment tools, most felt that the process helped them to ask better questions and to target candidates' development plans more effectively.

One CEO offers some practical advice on how to get the most out of the leadership assessment process: be picky about which assessment firm you partner with and which assessor you use. Ask the leadership development firm who their best assessor is (based on client feedback) and make sure you're working with the best person available. Like all professional services firms, every organization has different levels of talent and competence. In this case, the CEO ended up using an assessor with one of the top leadership consulting firms. Rather than work with a consultant from his own geographical area, the CEO used one from another market because she was considered the best in the field.

This CEO also recommends that you put yourself through the assessments before using them with your CEO succession candidates. That way, you can validate whether the results seem appropriate and, more importantly, you can compare your results to those of your potential successors. Such a comparison will spark lively discussion about how their executive leadership will differ from yours and whether the differences may be valuable or problematic to the firm.

Being Intentional about Leadership

Be Curious about People and Listen Attentively

Curiosity is defined as the strong desire to know or learn something. A curiosity mindset prompts inquiry, inquisitiveness, deeper listening and learning. Curiosity and fear offer two different perspectives on risk, two opposite ways for managing (or reacting to) uncertainty and the unknown.

As you talk to candidates, remember that they may have a fear mindset. It can be daunting talking to the CEO about their career hopes and dreams, no matter how confident people may appear outwardly. Candidates may be worried about what is lurking around the corner. Can they tell the truth? Will they be shut out?

To encourage open dialogue, be inquisitive. Focus on asking questions about what the candidates want to accomplish and what their hopes and dreams are, and then listen—really listen—to what they say.

Imagine yourself as a CEO who personifies curiosity. Would you be like a detective who doesn't know how his case will unfold, or like an investor doing due diligence on a new venture? Or would you be like a naturally curious child, asking questions with an open mind, almost with no bounds? How you ask the questions is as important as the questions you ask.

As one former CEO observed:

> You have to challenge CEOs to really hold up the mirror. Ask them: Are you the kind of CEO people feel comfortable talking to? Do people feel respected in your presence? Are they open and ready to tell you the truth? If people are holding back, you can't assume this reflects *someone else's* development gap. It could just as easily be your own.

Acknowledge Political Agendas and Encourage a Win-Win Exchange

Capitalism is rooted in the belief that serving one's self-interest is a catalyst for innovation and growth. This self-interest is alive and well in corporations. Historically, it was common for executives to get bonuses based on their individual performance ratings or for corporate profits to have priority over employee benefits or environmental impacts. But when it comes to CEO succession, as soon as stakeholders focus on "my interest" versus "your interest," there are problems.

In our view, CEO succession is not binary. It cannot be about serving one person over another. This simply doesn't work. There must be a win-win exchange. As soon as one person puts their self-interest above the needs of someone else, politics open. Issues go underground. Ego plays unfold.

As the sitting CEO, you can stir up these politics by focusing too much on your own needs or on the company's interests during the exchange. Several of the CEOs we interviewed made comments related to this. They said that when the CEO showed up more interested in them than in the company, they noticed and they felt recognized and valued. They also said that when the CEO was truly curious about their life and gave freely of his or her time, it built their confidence in the process; they felt that the process was about finding win-win solutions for the company's needs and their own. Contrast this to the CEO who spends 80 percent of the time talking about the company or his or her own needs or, worse yet, conveying the message through subtle behaviors that it is unlikely anyone in the future can do the job better than he or she has done.

It's good also for you to be aware of how candidates can stir up politics, so that you can watch out for it. For candidates, the politics arise when they see the CEO role as part of a career game, a push for status or an ego booster. If becoming the CEO is a way to maximize their "personal score" at work or in life, a means of knocking opponents out of the running or as solely about making more money, it becomes a problem sooner or later.

In our view, the CEO job requires a focus on creating real long-term value for the business and for others and it requires respecting and striving to meet others' needs. Doing this necessitates strong emotional intelligence and a leadership compass rooted in performance and relationship values. When candidates show up focusing on their ego's interests, you have to wonder what will happen when they become the CEO.

Be mindful that fear is inevitable with CEO succession. Fear is different from an ego play, even though sometimes the behaviors look similar. The fear isn't negative; it's a sign that people care about their careers and the work they do. Yet it's real and it can be destructive if not talked about openly and the concerns addressed.

Test Your Listening Skills

- When was the last time you had a career conversation with your most important team members?
- Do you know their career aspirations?
- Do you know what is happening with them outside of work?
- Do they feel respected in career conversations?
- Do they feel invited to take some risks?
- Do they feel supported to grow their skills and career?
- How much time do you typically spend giving advice and talking in these meetings?

Manage Expectations. Avoid False Promises.

As soon as you tell a candidate that they are being considered for a future CEO role, you must concurrently manage their expectations. Managing candidate expectations is one of the most difficult—and often frustrating—aspects of CEO succession planning. It has to start from the very first conversation if you want to prevent turmoil later.

It may sound almost too simple, but the best way to manage expectations is to educate candidates on the reality of the situation about when and how a CEO will be selected and about who will make the decision and on what basis, and to keep the lines of communication open. This helps you avoid creating false promises.

While it would be dangerous to ever tell a candidate they were guaranteed to get the job, they may infer it from your actions. We worked with a client who told their top CEO contender five years in advance that he would get the job. A lot can happen in five years! A better approach is to tell the candidate that your role is to set him or her up for success so that when the vacancy opens up, they will be in a great position to compete for the job: the rest is up to them.

Like so many aspects of being the CEO, you need to be an excellent communicator when working with candidates. They want the personal touch. They want more communication, not less. When communication drops off it can feel like a "dark hole," "paralyzing," and "awkward." (These are the words of CEO candidates who subsequently became CEOs, not ours.)

As one CEO in financial services said:

Sometimes not knowing where you stand is a good thing. It allows you to look back and reflect and think about what you have done to succeed and what you haven't done. But if it goes on for too long, it chips away at your confidence.

And, of course, if you don't manage expectations well it becomes problematic when you eventually promote someone else into the role. Imagine if you were told you would get a promotion to CEO, only to have the position pulled out from under you at the last minute. Imagine what it would be like walking into a CEO job if half your new direct reports thought they deserved the role and were passed over without proper consideration. Awkward! This happened to one CEO we interviewed. It took him six months of authentic (and tough) conversations to clean up the carnage.

⊙ Communication in Critical Moments

To Share the CEO Succession List, or Not?

Should you publish the succession list or keep it private? Should people know if they are a contender or not? How many people should be on the list? All good questions; all political landmines.

We believe that your CEO succession list should be about half a dozen candidates. As one CEO from financial services said:

> If you have more than six CEO candidates, you have a list of people that need leadership training, not a CEO succession list. A list this size will backfire under board scrutiny.

We recommend that you share the potential CEO successor list with the board's succession committee and no one else. Rather than show candidates "the list," tell them where they stand and what they need to do to progress. They will probably figure out who else is on the list based on who is getting plum developmental assignments, but they don't need to be told explicitly who their competition is.

We acknowledge that some CEOs have a different view.

They tell candidates who else is on the list to generate what they referred to in our interviews as "some healthy competition." One CEO, who runs a competitive and sales-oriented company, wanted everyone on his list to know who their competition was. As he put it, "I told people they were on the list and watched them campaign."

However, the CEO candidates we talked to who went through these types of competitive scenarios did not appreciate the experience. One CEO who was subjected to this sort of race (and won) reflected:

> Being part of a horse race was not a helpful or positive process. I would recommend that a few candidates be identified early and that you involve them in conversations about what it would be like to run the company at this level, and then give them time to try out the job and take on key experiences that reflect what the job is all about. As I develop my own successor, I am being more nurturing. My experience was sudden and jarring, and if it didn't turn out so well for me, it could have been challenging.

With either approach, be mindful of how your lists get circulated. In one situation, we had a client find out he was a CEO candidate because he was on the distribution list for an executive meeting. He received a spreadsheet with his name on it, along with a list of all his weaknesses. No one had told him he was being considered as a CEO candidate or that the level of his strategic acumen was seen as a potential barrier to career progress. You can imagine how he felt when he got the news in his in-box!

Political Pitfalls

Watch Out for the Golden Child

Once you identify candidates and start to develop them, others in the business will take notice. The upside to this approach is that it reinforces a developmental culture and shows others you personally value and invest in career growth. There is also a common downside: creating "golden child" status. This happens when others perceive the extra attention given to candidates as negative. In one CEO's case, her peers struggled with this and were jealous. They called her "the chosen one." Competition set in and they began to make derogatory comments. Think about how difficult it was for her. To avoid this in your business, she recommends giving each of your executives a development plan rather than singling out any one person.

A Career Coach May Be Your Biggest Ally

Should you hire an executive coach to have career conversations with CEO succession candidates? Several CEOs we spoke to said they gave candidates an opportunity to work with an executive career coach before having an official meeting to discuss their interest in the CEO role. Having an external coach as a sounding board helped the potential candidates to clarify their goals and whether or not they wanted the CEO job. They worked through their fears and identified their gaps in a confidential manner before officially communicating their interest and development gaps.

 **In Summary**

Plan to have candid conversations with potential candidates, setting aside time for these career conversations. Be curious about each candidate and listen attentively to them rather than trying to respond to every comment. Recognize that candidates may fear these conversations; think of your own experiences when you were a candidate facing crucial conversations with the CEO and the board. Manage the candidates' fears by tapping into the whole person in your discussions, considering what really motivates them. Consider using a variety of methods to assess candidate readiness, from one-on-one conversations to company-wide talent pools. Use leadership assessments to deepen your questions and learn about the candidate's potential derailers. Be careful how you manage the political dynamics related to sharing CEO succession lists. Clearly, preparing for and having conversations about your succession can be challenging for both you and the candidates. You have to be prepared not only during the actual process but also mentally, so you show up as a strong and confident leader. To help you get started on this important aspect of CEO succession planning, we offer some self-coaching questions.

? Self-Coaching Questions

- If talent development is a high priority for your organization, does it occupy an important part of your agenda as CEO?

- Have you asked the candidates you're grooming how you can help them develop their leadership skills?

- Have you asked whether they want the CEO job and have you really listened to their responses with a curiosity mindset?

- If you were a potential candidate, how much involvement and personal time would you want from the CEO in your development program?

- Are you avoiding tough decisions about building the skills and capabilities of your top team and potential candidates? About making changes to your top team if needed to support this development?

- What's your philosophy on leadership assessments? Are there merits to putting all your executives through the process, including yourself? Or only CEO candidates?

- What's your approach to transparency for the CEO succession list: to tell or not to tell? How public do you want the information to be? Have you thoroughly considered the impact this might have on the candidates?

- Is there consensus on what candidate-identification process you will follow?

4

BE RESULTS-
ORIENTED:
COACH AND
DEVELOP OTHERS

Key Leadership Quality

Be results-oriented. Coach and develop others. Set people up for success. Hold people accountable for making progress on their development plan.

I sat down with the CEO every so often to discuss my development plan. He seemed distracted and I felt he wanted to rush through this discussion. It gave me the impression he did not care and that my future was limited.

N OW THAT you have identified your CEO candidates, it's time to develop them.

If you're tempted to throw your CEO candidates off the deep end to see if they can "sink or swim" because that is what happened to you, we recommend that you think again. Although this was the approach ten or twenty years ago, times have changed. And in reality, the good old days were not always that good for everyone. It also won't work well if you create a development plan and then look at it a year later or if you send candidates on a content-heavy course and simply hope for the best. This is an ongoing process that requires continual attention.

Today, the overarching attitude for modern companies is that developing CEO potential and running the business are a single pursuit. Look around the business and ask yourself: what needs to be done here? Then give your CEO candidates a series of diverse experiences and carefully selected job assignments that stretch them and get the most important work done. With this delegation approach, candidates get the chance to develop their skills, and you implement your business strategy. As a bonus, candidates will feel stretched and challenged, keeping them motivated and fully absorbed in their work while you free up some of your time for other activities.

We asked our interviewees: What are the best types of formative experiences for CEO candidates? What experiences prepare them to become a CEO? The results are shared in this chapter.

We also give you ideas on how to coach and mentor effectively and how to develop leaders throughout your business so you have a pipeline of leaders ready to progress, not just candidates for the CEO role.

What Successful CEOs Do

Proactively Create Opportunities for CEO Candidates to Develop

When we asked current CEOs to share the formative experiences that best prepared them to take on their role, we heard four consistent themes:

- Getting experience setting a vision and taking full responsibility for delivering results, ideally in a fast-changing environment
- Taking on a broader span of control by running multiple operations or multi-functional business units
- Gaining exposure to the board/investors
- Practicing impulse control, especially when in the hot seat

Each of these themes is discussed in more detail below.

Vision Setting

Every CEO we spoke with said that a key formative experience was being given challenging, complex and strategically relevant job assignments. To accomplish this, they were given complete responsibility for setting the vision, making it happen and delivering the desired outcomes. The best types of experiences are high-stakes projects for the business that include things like deciding on the company's direction in the marketplace, taking on a turnaround project or a major strategic initiative or updating and implementing a new business model for a key product or service line.

Each of these assignments becomes a learning point, a chance for the candidates to grapple with challenges and for you to coach and mentor them. They serve as thresholds for development, pushing and helping the candidates see how their leadership needs to evolve to meet the broader demands of a CEO role. When taking on these assignments, it's common for candidates to get lost in their old habits or ways of doing things that served them in more limited roles. Each assignment is a chance for them to see how they habitually approach things and to figure out where they may need to adapt their style and approach. Although delivering on outcomes is the crux of the CEO job, ultimately it's *how* a candidate delivers on the outcomes and what leadership styles they employ that set future CEOs apart from the rest.

As CEO candidates take on job assignments, it's important that all parties know what success looks like so that there is a goalpost to strive for and coach toward. As one CEO we spoke with pointed out, this is a shared responsibility:

> When I was being groomed for the CEO job, I appreciated that the company deliberately carved out some development assignments for me—opportunities for

me to lead a change and deliver on a vision, with multiple operations under my belt. But if I were faced with doing this for my successor, I would take it one step further. I would clarify what the candidate needs to deliver on to show their CEO potential. I would clearly lay out my expectations about what success looks like and be sharper in my approach. I would also encourage the candidate to ask for more clarity. This is good preparation for doing the CEO job; they will have to constantly define the goalposts and make sure the stakeholders are clear on what is being delivered.

Broader Control over Multiple Operations or Functions

Another formative experience is running multiple operational areas or multi-functional business units. Running a larger site opens candidates' eyes to the reality that they need to let go and be more values-driven in order to succeed. As the span of responsibility increases, candidates can no longer place high importance on being the star who delivers outcomes solo. Instead they have to place greater value on leading through others, setting up others for success and letting go. They have to shift their lens to thinking about the "whole" organization, not just one functional area. As one CEO candidate said, "I had to shift from a *me* to a *we* mindset pretty darn fast."

These broader job assignments allow you to see whether candidates are getting stuck in an individually focused stance or whether they are setting teams up for success and influencing company-wide outcomes.

Exposure to the Board/Investors

It's vital for CEO candidates to get exposure to the board or investors. With the current trend toward boards becoming more professional and board governance getting stronger, the relationship between your future CEO and the board will likely be more valued and important than during your tenure. To prepare candidates, give them an opportunity to present their strategies to the board, report on outcomes, build relationships and endure the hot seat when challenged.

However, don't just limit their board exposure to little snippets of interaction; give them full exposure. One former CEO we spoke with, who is now on multiple boards, advises:

> Many CEOs give their successors the opportunity to present to the board, but they don't give them full exposure to board meetings. In my view, this is a mistake. Navigating the board is one of the most difficult parts of being a CEO. It's helpful for CEO candidates to see how meetings run from end to end, how decisions are made, the kind of questions that come up and how the current CEO handles this.

It's also helpful for CEO candidates to see the subtleties of the board, not just the mechanics (meeting schedules, reporting requirements, etc.). Give them exposure to how decision-making plays out by showing them which directors are strongest on particular types of issues, which ones are more engaged and which ones are more independent in their thinking.

When giving CEO candidates exposure to the board, view each meeting as a "coaching moment": review what happened and come up with strategies for being stronger for the next meeting. Whatever you do, don't undermine candidates by over-talking them or letting board members keep referring to you.

In this vein, one CEO candidate we spoke with compared his former boss (whom he couldn't stand) with his new boss (whom he raved about). His old boss asked him to present to the board on multiple occasions. Then she talked about him behind his back and withheld the board's feedback from him. She gave him the impression that she was saying one thing and doing another. Fast-forward a few years: his new boss was much more strategic, supportive and coach-like. Not surprisingly, with much better results, the candidate was eventually promoted to the CEO role. Here is his story:

> When I was being groomed for the CEO role, I was surprised by how much faith the CEO had in me. He made it clear that he knew my values were in the right place so he was comfortable with me making mistakes, yet he wouldn't hang me out to dry. For example, when he knew there were a few flaws in my argument, he would still allow me to present my ideas to the board so I could see how people took certain positions, and so I could learn from it.
>
> But right after key meetings, we did follow-up coaching and he would ask: What did you learn? What did you

see? How did you feel? The CEO was genuinely trying to help me through the experience and to learn. After I shared my view, he would say things like "Here are a few ideas for you to consider in the future," and "Here is what I recommend you consider as a follow-up." I quickly learned he had my back for the right reasons.

Another way to give them board exposure is to encourage CEO candidates to join an external board for a not-for-profit organization, preferably as the chair or vice-chair. Provided the board is run professionally, the experience gives candidates a strong reference point to draw on when they're in the CEO seat reporting to their own board. They will (hopefully) learn firsthand that board directors are often some of the most underused assets in an organization—a lesson that will help them, when the time comes, to capitalize on the smart, talented and dedicated people on their board.

Impulse Control in the Hot Seat

As a CEO, you can feel as if you're in the hot seat every day— and indeed you are in the hot seat—so it's important for CEO candidates to learn how to keep a healthy mindset and manage their behavior when under pressure. As one CEO said:

> When you're under pressure, being bombarded by people, asked to make high-stakes decisions in every meeting and being fully accountable for results that you don't have direct control over, it's easy for your mind to start playing tricks on you, especially when results are

going sideways. If you start having thoughts like "The people around me don't want me to succeed" or "They have it in for me," then you are finished. You have to have the guts to believe in yourself. And this is easier said than done, especially when you first get the job.

Call it mindfulness, self-awareness or impulse control, CEO candidates need to develop their "impulse control" muscles. This involves learning tactics for reading situations and people, staying calm and managing physical reactions, such as going red in the face or stammering, when someone pushes their buttons. It's learning how to uncouple behavior from emotion.

Typically, CEO candidates learn to get better at this through repeated exposure and working with an executive coach. In this area, external coaching often focuses on examining emotional triggers and unproductive beliefs and on learning to tap into the brief moments between a thought, an emotion and a behavior. Through training and practices, a CEO becomes like a surgeon performing a difficult operation: objective and focused on getting the job done, without letting emotional distress or anxiety get in the way.

Social Media and Developing an Online Reputation

CEOs of the future must understand how to navigate the world of social media and how to build and manage their online reputation. One tweet or a quick video shot from a distance can bring down reputations and goodwill. We recall one case of a prominent and highly successful CEO who was videotaped abusing a puppy in an elevator on his personal time. The video went viral and a few months later the board was forced to fire the CEO for his behavior. Consider offering training on how to use social media tools to advance the business, how to engage online and what to do in the event of an online crisis.

Coach and Mentor, Which Includes Giving Respectful, Real-Time Feedback

When developing CEO candidates, your role will primarily be that of an internal coach and mentor. In this context, this means helping them to resolve any difficulties and taking their game to the next level. It is not a soft activity, but is directly linked to working through explicit business needs and challenging candidates to think and lead differently.

Acting as an internal coach can, however, be difficult if you are the CEO. Because there is a reporting relationship, candidates may shut down so as not to limit their career. The critical skills required are asking the right questions at the right time, managing your impulses to dive into solutions, simply staying quiet and allowing candidates to develop their thoughts, and helping them to recognize they had the answers all along.

Published in 2016, Michael Bungay Stanier's book *The Coaching Habit* is a good resource for managers and leaders who recognize that they can be most effective as a leader by being an internal coach for their team. Stanier lays out a simple and effective habit-forming approach to internal coaching using seven key questions. We encourage you to pick up this resource and begin to use it with your executive team today—it might just help you find the time you thought you didn't have to help your people grow and build a more effective management team.

One of the challenges of being a coach to CEO candidates is knowing when to jump in and help and knowing when to hold back. One former CEO we interviewed shared a pearl of wisdom here. To help him assess the best approach to use, he would ask himself the question: "If I am totally invested in the candidate's success *and* the success of the company, what would I do here?" He found that this simple question kept him firmly in a win-win stance, revealing whether he needed to push for more or hold his tongue. For example, after years of building a strong company brand, he wasn't sure whether he should chime in and help his CEO candidate develop a marketing strategy or hang back, which he was tempted to do. But when he asked himself this question he knew he had to help. It wouldn't serve anyone if he didn't elevate the CEO's approach and share his point of view.

Another coaching matter is selecting valuable topics. For example, one important topic to address relates to developing allies in the business. Who will support candidates in their quest to become a CEO, and who might not? When coaching CEO candidates, we ask them to list six stakeholders they believe must support their candidacy and the extent to which they believe each of these people is already a supporter. This is a springboard for a powerful conversation about why people may be advocates or blockers and what to do about it. As the CEO you can take this conversation a step further by mentoring people to understand better key stakeholders' agendas and offering tips for relationship development. In an ideal world, your top CEO contender will be viewed as the obvious choice by everyone in the business, but to get to this point takes tremendous effort and effective coaching.

When coaching candidates, keep in mind that they crave this kind of attention. They want really good feedback that will help them to grow. Successful people want to know how they can be better. If you embed ongoing feedback and real-time coaching into your development assignments, you will help executives experience greater business success and personal happiness.

Brian shares his experience of being a CEO and leadership team coach within his organization:

As CEO I spent a lot of time and effort building the top team of the organization and part of this meant being a coach and mentor, with monthly one-on-ones and frequent check-ins. I was supported by my own executive coach and other limited resources. As I reflect back, there always seemed to be what I now call the "CEO barrier" that prevented accelerated learning. That barrier is the challenge of developing someone who reports directly to you as CEO.

After stepping down from the CEO job, I completed a coaching training program and continue to this day providing executive coaching as an external resource. With this new experience and training, I look back and see how I could have used many of these coaching tools and processes to support my top team and succession candidates, thereby breaking down that CEO barrier.

My advice to current CEOs is to take a few short courses on being an effective coach and to read about the processes that work for others, like those discussed in this chapter. Get help from your own executive coach who has this training and experience. The final step is to practice—a lot—as you will get better over time. You may find that being a better internal coach will open new doors of personal development for your successors and create a stronger succession plan and candidate pool. I think you will also enjoy doing it.

Develop Leaders Company-Wide, Not Just for the CEO Role

When you promote an executive into the CEO role, a vacancy shows up somewhere else, creating a domino effect. To generate bench strength, consider offering in-house executive development programs for all levels of leaders, not just the CEO. Although there are many ways you can design these types of programs, here are three high-impact approaches shared by our exclusive interviews with CEOs:

- put in place an executive cabinet
- develop an authentic leadership program
- support participant-led curriculum.

Executive Cabinet

Putting in place an executive cabinet is such a practical idea; we love it. Here's how it works. The CEO and succession committee identify the top five high-potential executives in the business: the people likely to be a CEO or a critical executive leader in the near future. These people may sit in an executive seat today, or they may not.

Together they become an executive cabinet, an independent structure (not necessarily part of regular reporting lines) that is a key contributor to business strategy and operations. As a cabinet they get exposure to business issues they would not otherwise be a part of, and they're able to see the complexity and opportunities for contribution. They might work on building blocks for growth or meaty issues that require the courage to rethink how the business operates. Working together, members of the cabinet strive for improvements at every corner of the company, weighing risks and opportunities.

This approach gives the business a chance to develop a number of CEO candidates at once, and it simulates the cross-functional teamwork needed in the top job. Also, emergency succession candidates often come from the executive cabinet, helping to manage succession risks.

Authentic Leadership Programs

One of the CEOs we interviewed described how they developed an authentic leadership program for their executives. They recognized that one of the struggles of leadership is daring to be real. In this program, each participant is asked to create a leadership compass—a simple tool that identifies their strengths, values and growth areas as a leader.

To create their compass, participants take a series of leadership assessments that review everything from personality to conflict skills, and they have sessions with an executive coach to identify their values and purpose and help them understand how their style helps or hinders their success.

A core tenet of the program is that being authentic is less about describing who you are than it is about showing people what you care about and value. To this end, each participant presents his or her compass to their peers, sharing stories that reveal their strengths, struggles and lessons learned along the way. Connection and growth happen through the exchange and through the truth of the stories, all culminating in deeper relationships and greater self-awareness.

Personal Leadership Compass

In our coaching business, we find that world-class leaders are guided by a set of personal values and are clear about what matters to them. This type of clarity is not automatic; it requires effort. If you want to clarify your guiding principles or refresh them, you can download the Leadership Compass tool we use with our clients. Download it on the companion website to this book: www.YourCEOSuccessionPlaybook.com.

Participant-Led Programs

Another approach is to have program participants design executive development programs themselves and then lead them. One company whose CEO we interviewed offers an executive development program focused on business acumen for their top twenty-five high-potential leaders. Participants in each cohort pinpoint what they want and need to learn, then they split off into teams to design the curriculum. Participants tend to get competitive with each other, becoming determined to offer a better learning experience than their peers from previous years.

For example, one year the participants wanted to learn about financial analysis, so they tracked down a top Wall Street analyst in their industry to teach them how to see the business through an analyst's eyes. Through this experience they picked up tips for competing, innovating and succeeding in their industry, and they learned how to reimagine their finances in order to stay ahead.

In another case, the participants wanted to learn how to accelerate their business dealings in China through joint ventures and foreign investment. To this end, participants toured their facilities and manufacturing sites in China, met with industry executives throughout East Asia to compare and contrast practices, and met with government officials and investors to improve understanding of the investment landscape. Although the trip was only two weeks long, it had a profound impact on how participants viewed business opportunities in Asia, influencing the company's business dealings for years to come. Through the experience, participants better understood the parallel universe of the Chinese Internet, the reality and implications of pollution and the types of opportunities that were being showered with money.

Clearly this company had a healthy budget, but the point is that participant-led leadership development programs provide a rich opportunity for grooming high-potential executives (and the approach takes some pressure off you to design it).

Being Intentional about Leadership

Review Candidates' Development Plans

As you develop candidates, keep in mind that being results-oriented matters. One CEO we spoke with (we'll call her Linda) gets top marks for holding her executives accountable for achieving their development plans and being results-oriented. For inspiration, we highlight her story here.

Linda is the CEO of a national company, and it's important to say that she is good at this now but she wasn't always so diligent in her approach. Early in her career she fell into the trap of rushing into development conversations sandwiched into a jam-packed schedule and being vague about what she really needed from people. Linda's style was to move so fast, it created limited opportunities for high-quality conversations. Based on feedback from an executive coach, she learned that her coaching and feedback sessions were viewed as superficial; she needed to be better. To improve, she created a system for developing others and she committed to implementing it diligently—an approach that is now a hallmark of her success as CEO.

Every quarter, Linda sets aside two days to meet one-on-one with her executives in order to review their development plans in detail and to offer coaching and mentorship. Since the development plans are linked to critical business needs, she is at the same time holding the team accountable for delivering toward the company goals. She does this in order to prepare high-quality feedback and offer strategies for taking each person's development to the next level, even going so far as soliciting input from the succession committee before she meets with each person. (As an aside, this shows the succession committee she is following through on plans, which builds their confidence also.)

Although the meetings lean toward learning and growth, a key message is that she expects results. Linda makes the assumption people are going to follow through and focuses her questions on what they learn along the way. When debriefing assignments, she regularly asks questions like: What did you expect to happen? What actually happened? What did you learn? How will this inform your approach moving forward?

Creating a regular schedule of accountability meetings embeds development into the culture, and it helps Linda to be "in the zone" when having these conversations. Because she tends to think and talk fast, she has to be deliberate about slowing down for the sessions. After years of refining her approach, she now believes that this is the best use of her time each and every quarter and that who she is being in the meeting transforms the tone. The tone isn't "get it done, or else." It's more like "What was done? What can we learn? What's next?"

In our view, the benefit of Linda's story is twofold. It reminds us that creating systems and habits can make a positive difference, leading to the results that matter, and that being a good mentor and coach takes practice. Following Linda's lead, it makes sense to review candidates' development plans as thoroughly and regularly as you review strategy and budgets and to pay attention to the tone you are setting.

⊙ Communication in Critical Moments

Share Your Own Story and Journey to Becoming the CEO

When coaching and developing candidates it can be tempting to jump in with career advice, thinking you are being helpful. Although there is value in good advice, consider sharing a story about your road to becoming a CEO instead. Although it requires some vulnerability on your part, it is one of the most powerful development tools at your disposal.

Natalie realized the full power of this approach through her work running CEO peer groups. During these sessions, she facilitates an exercise in which she asks the participants to share their story—the peaks and valleys of their career and life, and how those experiences have shaped them as a person and as a leader. The point of the exercise is to get a group of CEOs to bond through getting to know each other on a more human level. Each time Natalie facilitates this, she is moved and inspired by people's stories, as are the participants in the peer group.

The last time she ran this exercise, one CEO beamed as he shared the elation he felt from rising in his career. Another cried as he remembered the death of his child. Others shared stories from peaks in their life or from their darker days: the victory of selling a business; the birth of a child; confusion stemming from being fired; watching a business fall apart during a recession; choosing career over love and paying the price.

At the end of the exercise, one CEO of a global firm said:

Imagine if our employees heard these stories. They would be so surprised. I bet most people look at CEOs and think they achieved a straight line to the top. They don't realize what it takes to get there and that we all suffered through something.

He's right. Most people likely view you as the most confident person in the room, and they won't know and learn from your story unless you tell them. By sharing your experience, you create the sense that you're in the fray of business and life just like they are and that you are ultimately on the path of growth together. Through your story you make it clear: there is no straight line to the CEO job. Everyone has flaws, and all that projected confidence isn't always what it seems.

✖ Political Pitfalls

Confirmation Bias

As you develop candidates, keep in mind that bias can cloud your judgment. Once you have a "pick" or two in mind, you may naturally pay attention to positive information about these candidates and their potential and, conversely, avoid less favorable data. This doesn't happen on purpose. It's a cognitive bias—the confirmation bias—and it's quite common.

What's more, if others in the business believe you are highly invested in someone, they may stop giving you the straight goods about their performance and potential, thinking it's taboo to say anything bad about the future CEO, your so-called golden child. Candidates themselves may be less forthcoming about their development needs and personal struggles for fear of being perceived as no longer "CEO material." As the late Wayne Dyer once said, "When you change the way you look at things, the things you look at change."

To avoid this pitfall, apply all the insights provided in this chapter: focus on a learning culture, regularly solicit input from others, give feedback and be balanced in the candidate data you gather. At the first whiff of a cognitive bias, invite others to share information that contradicts your point of view.

 **In Summary**

Give candidates responsibility for a key business area so that they can develop a vision and strategy and lead a team to deliver results. Back away and let the candidates learn, make mistakes and be accountable for delivery. In candidates' development assignments, clarify the expectations for delivery and success. Let candidates demonstrate that they can deliver in multiple situations outside their current areas of responsibility. Mentor candidates on how to deliver success through others, as team-building is an important part of the CEO job. An external executive coach can add value in many situations. Help candidates interact with the board, investors or other key stakeholders so that they can experience being in the CEO's hot seat. Provide candidates with thoughtful feedback after their presentations and meetings. Ask open-ended questions and then share your insights; this provides a powerful learning experience. Find opportunities to discuss and share experiences on managing impulse control as a CEO. Let candidates practice on the executive team. Explore other methods to develop successors and decide which ones are appropriate for your company culture. Be aware of your personal biases. Encourage others to give you straightforward, honest feedback so that you remain open-minded and supportive.

To help guide your thinking about being more results-oriented as you coach and develop future leaders, we offer you the following self-coaching questions.

? Self-Coaching Questions

- To what extent do you have a win-win approach when developing CEO candidates?

- What formative experiences are best suited to your CEO candidates?

- What other development methods or assignments do you think your CEO candidates would benefit from?

- Do you have an accountability system to help drive results?

- Have you clearly articulated what success looks like for candidates' development assignments?

- What personal biases are alive and well in your organization today?

5

BE
THOUGHTFUL:
PROMOTE
WITH CARE

Key Leadership Quality

Be thoughtful. Promote with care. Show consideration for people's needs. Be attentive with your communication and your actions when transitioning to the next CEO.

A few minutes after I received the call from the board chair that I was selected for the CEO role, my phone lit up. The unsuccessful candidates were fishing for information, wanting to know who was selected. I immediately realized that the board chair had called me first and others were in the dark. Then it got messy. Here I was trying to build trust with them and retain them for my team, yet I couldn't say anything because I felt it was the chair's job to talk to them. What a first thirty minutes on the new job!

IT'S TIME to promote and transition to your successor. Showtime! If all goes well you will have a smooth hand-off. However, it's equally possible that the transition will be rife with politics.

In truth, every time you promote someone in the business, employees are paying attention to what you do and how you do it. They are evaluating whether people are promoted based on merit, favoritism or some other unwritten rule. One key message: don't get caught up in the to-do's and the checklists. The hand-off is about people, relationships and success. But how do you avoid the politics? What are the tools and strategies you need to be aware of?

Our experience has taught us that the best way to avoid negative politicking is to have a formal, visible and defensible process when promoting people into the CEO role—and actually, into all roles. To illustrate this point, think about recent political elections. When people believe that the democratic process is working, they can more readily accept election outcomes. When this is not the case, you can have a revolution!

As a key sponsor, you will want to be thoughtful about how you are promoting others so that the entire succession process has credibility and creates goodwill. This means your process must be well thought out, systematic and communicated effectively; you must follow through on what you say you will do.

Nevertheless, even if you are highly attentive to everyone and are a master communicator, there will still be some people who are disgruntled by the transition. Your best leadership attributes won't completely diminish the stress resulting from the change. But if you stay committed to these two principles—focusing on people and paying attention to their needs—the transition will have a much greater chance of going smoothly.

In this chapter, we offer you tips for staying focused on what matters during this phase so you can achieve a positive outcome and avoid politics. This involves everything from executing a first-rate CEO selection process to setting up the new CEO for success, all the while being sensitive to the politics of winners and losers. We also provide a sample communication for announcing the new CEO.

What Successful CEOs Do

Influence a Credible Selection Process

Let's face it, most board members don't have a lot of experience selecting a new CEO. They may go through this once or twice in their career at best, if ever. Like you, they are probably learning and doing as they go. This creates a tricky dynamic for you. Do you let them handle it and run the risk of its going sideways? Or do you jump in there and try to influence the process and outcome? The best-case scenario is that you are an influencer and a participant among the board members, guiding the process to the best outcome.

The first matter to influence is the design of the CEO selection process. As with all executive hires, you will want a well-planned process with milestones, clearly outlined communication and established roles. What you don't want is a poorly planned process where you change your course midstream and upset candidates. The worst is when you interview all your internal candidates, give them the impression they have a good chance of getting the role, then leave them hanging for months while you change course and decide to look for candidates externally. Even if this ends up ultimately with an internal hire, it will be upsetting and irritating.

A key part of your job is to influence the makeup of the selection committee and to advocate a thoughtful approach. Who should be on the committee? How many people? What politics may brew?

The selection committee typically includes board members, other key stakeholders, often (but not always) the outgoing CEO, and other influencers. A key decision is whether you want an external third party (like a search firm or consultant) to broker the process. Pay attention to subjective matters, loyalties and politics when picking the committee and consultant; if you don't, these dynamics can unduly influence the process. Consider who likes whom, who talks to whom on the sidelines, how candidates will perceive the committee picks and who are the "yes" people versus the contrarians.

The CEOs we spoke with said that the best selection processes had an independent board chair as the main point of contact who would explain the process and steps to candidates and handle negotiations. It's a nice touch when the search consultant checks in with each candidate before and after the interviews, diffusing some of the candidate's pressure and uncertainty.

One CEO cautioned that it's important to clarify HR's role on the selection committee or things can get messy. When he was being considered for the CEO position, HR was the main point of contact leading the candidate discussions and negotiations. This was inappropriate; it meant HR was negotiating their boss's compensation package. In this case, it was doubly political because the VP of HR gave the impression that he preferred the other candidate. Ideally HR helps with the process, tools and procedures, but does not lead candidate discussions.

In an extreme example from our interviews, one CEO shared their big selection committee blunder. They put one of the unsuccessful CEO candidates on the final selection panel. Throughout the panel interview the disgruntled executive sat with arms crossed, exuding negative energy, clearly upset that she was not a finalist herself—awkward!

When it comes time to do the interviews, it's best to focus on the must-have criteria in the CEO success profile and to use a variety of interview types and techniques (e.g., one-on-one sessions, panels, presentations about the vision for the company, dinners). Make sure the interviews are not limited to casual chitchat, which may happen when the board has known the candidate for many years. The selection committee should be well-prepared, having developed appropriately hard-hitting questions, and committee members should also give candidates a chance to ask their own tough questions. Consider sourcing feedback from outside contacts who have knowledge of the candidates—a strategy that provides a more divergent source of candidate intel and can be part of the recipe for success.

The offer stage is the time when things can go sideways and get political. Our research confirms that internal candidates are often at a disadvantage because search committees don't extend the same urgency and respect with regard to their salary and title negotiations as they do for external candidates who often get the red carpet treatment. Our interviewees expressed discontent about this and view it as a costly mistake.

One CEO described her strong frustration in this area:

Personally, I have been in the role for *six months* and I am still not clear on how compensation works. It feels like this piece is misaligned, and it has become an elephant in the room with the board chair. To me this has become a pain point, and it's unfortunate that our board chair is not showing leadership on this. The compensation conversations are typically a bit awkward. I believe the compensation plan needs to be laid out and shared, and a path provided around where compensation can go if results are achieved. I believe in the value of presenting "steps along the way" with the compensation, particularly for a first-time CEO.

Another CEO faced a similar situation:

Our compensation discussions were messy. Looking back, I wish we'd had a third party managing it. We were both nervous and we made some mistakes. I accepted the job before we even had compensation discussions! I wish that the CEO had said, "We did some research on comparable companies and this is how compensation will work." I had been with the company for twenty years and, although we had a lot of trust, it would have been wise for me to get outside advice. When I develop my successor, I will be transparent and explicit about what the CEO needs to deliver to make their money.

A third CEO who was already a double threat—master salesperson and inspiring leader—struggled with negotiations too. At the time of offer, the board chair was evasive about increasing his compensation, but with some perseverance they were able to find a win-win approach. He explains:

> When they offered me the job, they presented me with an offer that was below my expectations; they were not negotiable. After a few futile attempts, I asked: If you are not negotiable now, what are the results I need to get in the next six to twelve months to set the stage for another compensation discussion?

Bingo! They laid out their expectations and soon after he got more salary plus equity. This strategy worked out well for him; the equity he received translated into a sizable payout when the company was sold a few years later.

Negotiations about the job title can be similarly loaded. A CEO with ten years in the top job is troubled by how boards often handle title matters. He points out that when you call a new leader "President" and not "President and CEO," you're leaving out a piece of the strategic accountability. In his view, if there is a chair of the board and the CEO is responsible for strategy, then the hire should be given the title of President and CEO.

Career management is another lens here. A newly promoted CEO shares:

> I initially wanted the CEO title to satisfy my ego, yet in the end I also wanted it so I could better manage my career. The board wanted to call me President, but when I consulted with my advisors on this matter they told me to push hard for President *and* CEO. If I didn't have both titles, I would always have to explain that I was the one doing the strategy and that I report directly to the board.

In the best examples, an independent board chair is the chief negotiator who has the authority to negotiate the compensation package without having to go back to the board each time terms are discussed. The board chair is also the key point of contact for you, the departing CEO. The board needs to handle your package with the same care too, if they want the transition to be on a strong footing. A poorly designed earnout, a confusing departure plan or inattentive tax planning can quickly become thorns.

Questions to Help You Design Your CEO Selection Process

Before looking at a single résumé, have your search committee work through the following questions:

1 What do we want the candidate experience to be like?

2 Who are we going to include in the interview process, and why?

3 How many interviews will there be, and what style of interview will we use (one-on-one, panels, presentations)?

4 What questions will we ask? Will each interview focus on the same thing or different things?

5 Will we incorporate leadership assessments? If so, what will we evaluate?

6 Will we include internal and external contenders? Will we tell candidates who else is in the running?

7 Who will be the lead communicator with candidates, including when the final package is negotiated?

8 How much flexibility will we give the lead contact to negotiate the package so that we avoid delays going back and forth between the candidate and the board?

9 What's our communication plan? Who will deliver the news to the candidates who don't get the job?

10 When and how will we manage the hiring announcements within the executive management team, throughout our organization and externally?

Power Changes People:
The Value of Leadership Assessments

This story is about how one CEO's best-laid plans went awry and how, in hindsight, he wishes he had used third-party assessments during the selection of his CEO successor:

> We worked with this CEO candidate for years and we thought we knew him well, so we didn't bother with leadership assessments. But the promotion didn't work out. When he assumed the role of President, his behavior changed for the worse. In hindsight, we didn't do our due diligence or understand the candidate's true nature. Our conversations weren't right.

> If this former CEO could do it again, he would require an in-depth leadership assessment and a more comprehensive 360 assessment, including feedback from direct reports. He also would have had many more open and curious discussions with the candidate. His advice to you: don't assume you know how your successor will behave in the President/CEO job, even if you've worked with him or her for years and know him/her socially. Power changes people.

Help Launch the Newly Promoted CEO

Aside from the usual orientation plan, there are three practices that give new CEOs exponential return during the hand-off phase. Encourage the new CEO to try these out: make a bold leadership statement, speak your truth with the board and do a listening tour.

Make a Bold Leadership Statement

It's important for the CEO-elect to communicate that they won't try to emulate you—they will do things their own way. People will be curious: What are the values and principles that matter to the new CEO? Are these values real or leadership clichés? What difference does this CEO want to make? They will wonder: Given what the new CEO is promising, do I want to work for them?

When the new CEO steps into their role, they will want to be proactive about declaring what they stand for by making a statement about their leadership. This can be profound because people will have high expectations of the new CEO, some expressed and some unspoken. Making a statement about leadership helps people discern whether they want to work with the new CEO and what might be on the other side of the hand-off.

One trailblazing CEO went beyond just words for her leadership statement. She wanted to show staff that things would be different under her leadership: more progressive and modern. To make this statement, before her first day on the job, she redecorated her new office (the CEO suite), changing it from old-fashioned to a more modern and inviting style. This may sound trivial, but it wasn't. The stylish furnishings and the creation of a lounge area were a clear kickoff to her new direction. On her first day a number of veteran employees enthusiastically noted: "We can see things will be different around here!"

Equally valuable learning comes from CEOs who were too timid and didn't make a bold leadership statement out of the gate. One CEO said he wouldn't make this same mistake again. To new CEOs he advises: "Don't doubt yourself, speak up." Here's his story:

> When I was a new CEO, I didn't fully realize the weight of having full responsibility for the business, [or] the power of my influence. As I got into the role, I was surprised that I would say something and people would respond so quickly. In hindsight, I would have been more deliberate about navigating this. I would have come up with some key leadership principles; not statements on the wall, but key principles I could build my reputation around. I would communicate this and put effort into behaving in ways that are consistent.

Speak Your Truth with the Board

For the new CEO, getting on the right foot with the board—fast!—is key. In our opinion, there's no better person to talk about this than one of the serial CEOs we interviewed who now chairs three boards. Originally an operations guy, his track record is running billion-dollar companies, and you can just tell he loves to lead. (We think he misses being a CEO.)

Here is his advice on this matter:

When I first started as CEO, I asked for some goals. The board said, "Grow the company." I pushed for more. "Grow in what areas? What are the key success measures? Who needs to agree?" To me, ambiguity is a death sentence. I have strong views on this. When starting the job, I do not want to simply jump into the middle of the outgoing CEO's plan and hope for the best. I will push for workable goals. I want to start fresh and have renewed clarity, even at the risk of being annoying.

He goes on to say:

A new job is like crunch time at school. It's time to put the extra effort in because your grade counts. To me, this means shining the light on relationships. I make the point of meeting with every board member in the first sixty days, some of them twice. I want to know where the synergies are, what people believe about the future and whether they support my candidacy. It's not enough to meet quarterly; I communicate way more than usual in the first year.

Getting to know individuals on the board on more than a superficial level and initiating a relationship of trust with each board member is as productive as the extent to which both parties are candid and clear in their communication.

Do a Listening Tour

On a related note, virtually every CEO we spoke to for this book suggested that the incoming CEO do a listening tour as part of the first one hundred days in the job. The listening tour is a pointed exercise in which the CEO travels to all the business units to listen to key stakeholders (not just the board) in order to understand the opportunities and uncertainties facing the business. The CEO then uses this input to formulate his or her plans to refresh the business strategy, with the added bonus of modelling a consultative approach.

What follows are the lessons learned and specific tips that the CEOs we spoke to shared: ways to turn a common practice into a high-performance toolkit.

- Use the listening tour to get a solid baseline of where you're at: "If you want to build a skyscraper, make sure you know what the foundation is made of."
- Connect with the top-ten customers: "Make sure you understand the end-to-end customer experience and think about whether it is compelling enough to keep the company strong in the future."
- Take a long, hard look at cash: "Pay close attention to what is most important for the financial health of the business, short-term cash flow, sales, margins and debt."
- Spend a day going through every social media channel out there, especially if customers write reviews online: "Find out what the company brand really means."
- Meet with as many people as possible: "I met with every single person in the company because I didn't want an internal coup when I was promoted."

- Use data from the listening tour when you prepare your go-forward strategy: "The insights you gain will be fascinating and, unless you plan on doing all the work yourself, they will be critical for getting buy-in later on."

Put in Place External Support to Bolster the Chances of Success

Another area for you to influence is investing in external support for the new CEO. Why? Because it's time for the new CEO to bust out of their comfort zone. But that doesn't mean settling for sleepless nights, knots in their stomach and feeling as if they're doing this all on their own. It helps to have connection with a close-knit external network.

There are four high-impact options revealed in our interviews: CEO boot camp, CEO peer groups, executive coaching and team coaching.

CEO Boot Camp

The CEO boot camp is a focused training and development program to equip new CEOs to tackle the myriad challenges and intense scrutiny they face in their early days. Think: exercise boot camp. In this case, CEOs put concentrated effort into topics such as bridging the gap between strategy and execution, building high-performance teams and accomplishing more in their first one hundred days than most

CEOs do in six months, all the while conducting in-depth self-examination. After an immersion experience on what it takes to be a high-performing CEO, participants are better prepared to take on the top job and to be more effective leaders overall.

The boot camp mentioned most often in our interviews was the Chief Executive Institute, a program offered by Korn Ferry International for newly promoted CEOs and their executive teams. In the program, participants work with a team of professionals for twelve to eighteen months to create a shared purpose in their business, drive value and get a strong start. Boot camps are led by current and former CEOs as well as specialists in human resources, business operations and financial matters. With a laser beam focus on the executive team, each participant works through a critical question: what would be possible in your organization if your executive team were fully engaged with a shared purpose?

Others we interviewed opted for similar executive education programs in top universities, including Stanford, INSEAD and Harvard.

CEO Peer Groups

CEO peer groups are another external resource for up-and-coming (and established) CEOs. A peer group typically consists of up to fourteen non-competing CEOs who come together to discuss their toughest business challenges and the personal toll of being a CEO. In this confidential forum, participants put a strategic issue on the table, get help and advice from their peers and learn from other CEOs about what to do (and what not do) based on others' experiences in similar situations.

As the cliché goes, it can be lonely at the top. One irony is that the better job the CEO does, the lonelier it can get. However, with a peer group it doesn't have to be that way. When CEOs hear each other out, help each other solve sticky strategy issues and inspire each other to be courageous, it can make all the difference in the world. Several of our interviewees saw their peer group as their lifeline during the transition. As one newly appointed CEO said, "With a peer group you realize there is such a high professional standard in the top ranks that it inspires you to raise your game." Another commented: "It was the one place I could get frank feedback about my strategy and approach. If I needed to hear it, my CEO peers would tell me I was nuts, when no one else would."

There are many different peer group organizations with different value propositions. Among the CEOs we interviewed, the most popular peer group organizations were MacKay CEO Forums (Natalie is a MacKay CEO Forums Chair in Vancouver), YPO and TEC/Vistage. There are also many peer groups organized by industry associations. (Brian chairs a group of CEOs for employee-owned professional services companies.)

Hire an Executive Coach

You may want to recommend the new CEO get an executive coach for the transition period. We have found this to be one of the best times to coach CEOs, as they are keen at the outset of their new appointments to self-reflect and especially to examine their leadership habits. Due to the emotions and stress of the CEO transition, every day is like a personal growth lab.

Natalie's specialty is to coach newly promoted executives and CEOs. Following is a case study to show you how coaching adds value during the transition period.

One of Natalie's clients (we'll call him John) was the new CEO of a company with about $100 million in revenue and offices across North America. Soft-spoken yet intense, John was promoted to CEO from the CFO position. The promotion was an important inflection point for him; he was shifting from peer to boss after a decade of working with the top team.

A key success factor in John's coaching was Natalie's proactively seeking advice from people John respected in the business to elicit suggestions for how he could reach his goals. Natalie interviewed ten people whom the new CEO respected; these included investors from the New York private equity firm that had a large ownership in the business, as well as top executives on the leadership team. In the end, it was clear John needed to shift his leadership style to drive results, position himself as the new leader among his peers and find his voice so he could stand his ground with the founder and private equity firm.

The interview feedback, described in a report, offered tangible ideas for growing the business, in addition to strategies that could improve John's leadership. When John received the report with the feedback, he wrestled with it, at times wanting to shove the information under the rug. His big "aha moment" was that he hesitates; he overthinks. This was going to get in his way during the transition. He needed to be more visionary and decisive. Upon reflection, he said, "This advice is not career gold, it is platinum."

John was courageous enough to look at his blind spots and smart enough not to get bogged down in them. The team needed him to state his vision, take decisive action with the underperforming team members, quickly mobilize the team around common goals and show the private equity firm he understood that the number-one company priority was growing sales and profit.

During the coaching John reframed how he leads. Instead of seeing himself as a leader who had to get his decisions right, he viewed himself as someone who could touch lives and mobilize action. This was a big stretch for him. He was a numbers guy at his core. But he worked through it, really honing in on board and executive meetings and setting the goal to inspire people with his vision during every meeting. Throughout the period of coaching he defined "his way" as a CEO, realizing that his signature style was to focus on relational trust first and decisive action second. Pausing to think helped him to do that, but he learned that how he communicated *before and after* the pause distinguished whether others perceived it as hesitation or strategic reflection.

At the end of a coaching engagement we measure results in target areas by talking again to the key interview stakeholders to gauge improvements. In our experience, when clients start a coaching process knowing they will be reassessed at the end of the engagement, they try harder because they know they will be held accountable.

In the end, John felt the coaching was an important contributor to his personal success and, in turn, to the overall success of his team and the company. The board chair was impressed with John's proactive approach to seeking input during the transition. The private equity firm believed they had made the right choice with the CEO hire, and they were pleased with John's performance and the company's financial success. Today the company and team are still growing strong.

Coach the Team

Most transition plans focus on boosting the skills and leadership of the CEO-elect, yet this emphasis perpetuates the idea that the CEO is an individual performer. One way to help the CEO-elect capitalize on the fresh start is to help him or her build a high-performing team. A coach for the entire team can aid the CEO-elect by diagnosing the team's current dynamics. The coach can ask important questions such as: What do we need to change to achieve our strategy? What are our dysfunctional patterns? What's it going to take for us to change our behavior?

A team coach can help the CEO surface the important discussions and pinpoint how the team needs to be led to take it forward. We find it typically takes a team about a year to really gel with a new CEO, yet with a team coach it often takes less than six months. Coaching amplifies the positive energy that comes with a new CEO and nips the negativity before it spreads.

Let Go to Add Value

Creating space for the new CEO to lead is obviously important; it requires you, the outgoing CEO, to let go. In his book *Succession: Are you Ready?* Marshall Goldsmith, with keen insight, described the letting-go dynamic in this way: "Almost all the leaders I have met assure me that they will be different. They confidently assert that they will have no problems letting go. You are probably delusional enough to believe that you too will be different. Take my word for it: while your desire for uniqueness is theoretically possible, it is statistically unlikely."

In 2009 when Brian was transitioning out of his job as President of Golder Canada to become President and CEO of the corporation, he struggled with letting go. On his worst days he got too involved in decisions that were now the responsibility of the incoming leader, who naturally was doing things his own way. Thankfully Brian had a strong enough relationship with the new regional president (someone he had worked with and mentored) that the latter could respectfully ask Brian to please back off, which he did to everyone's benefit. Others are not so lucky. The dynamics of letting go can lead to politics, turf wars and tough conversations.

Oftentimes, leaders who find it difficult to let go fit one of the two "types" outlined below.

1. The Career Lifer

If you have your identity wrapped up in your role or you have built your whole career with one company, you may find it more difficult to let go. For "lifers," leaving the company can feel like breaking up with a deep love or like losing a part of themselves. It makes you wonder: who am I without this job?

If this is your situation, be aware that you may inadvertently create politics by holding back information or handing over key relationships incompletely, keeping yourself positioned as the strategic authority. This confuses people and typically leads to secret whispers at the water cooler about when you are finally going to let the new CEO lead.

2. The Rainmaker

If you have been the person to bring in sales, and clients love you, it will be harder to let go, especially if you have not systematically built up your sales bench strength or transferred over accounts to people long in advance. If you are the rainmaker, watch for the "hero mindset." Your ego will try to trick you that the company can't survive without you, that you represent the gold standard of performance and that there is no one "out there" who can do it better. This can lead to never-ending comments about the future CEO, such as "He/she is not quite there yet," leaving the impression that the incoming CEO is second-best to you. Watch out: it can temporarily be like a badge of honor to feel indispensable, but it only leaves you in the lurch later on.

CEOs who have a more productive mindset will proactively groom a successor, introduce the successor to key people and express confidence in him or her, especially leading up to the transition. They recognize that part of their legacy is leaving someone strong to fill their shoes and setting this person up for success.

Although it is counterintuitive, one way to let go is to be clear about what you are going to stay involved with. In their January 2011 article in *McKinsey Quarterly* ("Making the Most of the CEO's *Last* 100 Days"), Christian Caspar and Michael Halbye suggest that rather than step back and avoid major decisions—a common instinct—you make a list of what you will stay involved with during your last one hundred days and communicate this clearly. The goal is to clean up any leftover issues so that the new CEO has a clean slate. Caspar and Halbye recommend you consider the following questions:

- What do I wish I'd understood better when I began the job?
- What's my plan for my last one hundred days on the job?
- If I had three more years in the job, would I make any big strategic or organizational shifts?
- Which difficult decisions about people would I make now if I were staying another three years?

- Does the business have the operational momentum it will take to deliver strong results this year and next year?

Caspar and Halbye suggest that while many might view such actions as intruding on the successor's territory, they have observed that when CEOs take a structured approach to their last days, it has been an invaluable gift to the incoming CEO.

Another approach is to create a transition agreement with the new CEO. Come up with five to eight commitments for the transition that you both agree to, and define how you will work together to activate them. Rather than make assumptions about the incoming CEO's needs, ask the new CEO how he or she wants you to contribute, if at all. Communicate clearly the areas where you believe working together in the transition stage can add the most value to the company in the long run.

When letting go, also consider physically getting out of the office. One CEO we spoke with took a four-month leave of absence as soon as the new CEO took over. His message to his successor was: "I will meet with you anytime, but not at the office. If you are on track after four months, then I will move into a director role on the board." Looking back, he realized this was a smart decision. If he had kept showing up at the office, staff would have drawn their own conclusions, and likely erroneous ones, about why he was there.

When departing CEOs have trouble letting go, it can lead to friction. One incoming CEO we interviewed expressed frustration that the departing CEO would not let go. Rather than pass over responsibilities, he opted to stay involved in strategic planning meetings, ostensibly to support his successor. Said the incoming CEO, "The transition was rocky, as it appeared that the former CEO did not want to leave." It got to be too much when the departing CEO showed up at a strategic planning meeting unannounced. "I had to ask him to leave. This was hard, but necessary." Notably, when we interviewed the departing CEO in question, he didn't discuss the incident. Instead he recollected his transition as "smooth and successful." It is amazing how people can have a different perspective on the same experience.

Being Intentional about Leadership

Be Thoughtful

We heard several stories of how important it is for you, the outgoing CEO, to show confidence in your successor during the inaugural period. It is the time to exhibit a real people-focus, showing your genuine support for the incoming CEO. This is different from saying "Congratulations, the board made a great hire." When you show *genuine support* the new CEO is touched and finds it meaningful; it becomes part of your departing legacy.

One newly appointed CEO was particularly moved by the departing CEO's gestures and support. As part of the hand-off, the outgoing leader hosted a dinner at his home, inviting all of the executives and their spouses so that he could publicly declare his support. The new CEO recalled:

> At the dinner, the departing CEO talked about his confidence in me and how excited he was to pass the leadership of the company to me. He then gave me a plaque, which included a newspaper clipping highlighting a meaningful story about one of our competitors, with the inscription: "Game on, you will win." It was these subtle things that showed me I had his full support, and this meant a lot, especially in front of my wife.

The value of symbolic gestures, like the plaque, showed up frequently in our interviews. These actions seem to touch people's hearts in ways that words cannot.

Here's another example which occurred in an international manufacturing company. The incoming CEO shared a symbolic moment with the outgoing CEO, whom the new CEO describes as the best mentor in his career:

> In my first all-staff meeting, we were asked a question about the future of the company. Normally I would sit back and let the [departing] CEO answer it, but he

wouldn't let me default to him. Instead, he handed the microphone to me. As I took the microphone it was a moment for both of us. The training wheels came off.

What's fun about symbolic gestures is they can work both ways. They help to honor the departing CEO too. For example, in the manufacturing company described above, the new CEO marked the outgoing CEO's departure by naming the main boardroom after him; this was rolled out with great fanfare and a party. A plaque honoring his contribution is still on the wall today. Another new CEO set up a company scholarship in honor of the departing CEO to acknowledge her contribution.

Of course, not all departing CEOs are worthy of such praise and recognition, but even when they're not, it pays to be thoughtful. An incoming CEO from the public sector was in the unfortunate position of replacing a lackluster CEO. He consciously spoke positively about the departing CEO so people understood that when someone leaves the organization, they are still respected. He didn't want employees to think that when they left the team, they would be talked about negatively. There is wisdom here.

◯ Communication in Critical Moments

Announcing the New CEO

Announcing the new CEO is a delicate process for sure: Do you keep the promotion under wraps until the last minute? Announce it months in advance? Who needs to be in the know? Who will be surprised or maybe even upset?

The worst-case scenario occurs when the announcement is poorly thought out, especially for the candidates who applied and were unsuccessful. It's embarrassing for CEO contenders to hear about the CEO-elect in public ways, such as when they come out of a meeting and a colleague greets them in the hall and says, "Sorry you didn't get the job." (*What? I didn't?!*) It's like being cut from the team in a publicly shaming way. Be caring here. Be human. Have a communications strategy. Think about people and the impact on their confidence and, ultimately, on their productivity.

There are two common approaches to the announcement of a new CEO:

- announce it a few months in advance so people can get used to the idea, or

- announce it at the last minute and move to swift action.

With both approaches the communication must include why the transition is happening, what it means for the future and why you are leaving. On a personal level, you will need your sound bite. Have your narrative about why you are leaving worked out and ready to be delivered.

Announce It a Few Months in Advance

Announcing the CEO in advance evokes confidence and a sense of order. It respects that everyone needs time to get used to the idea; this includes the marketplace and key candidates. Stakeholders won't be shocked—"Surprise, we have a new CEO!"—because with this approach, they are given a month or more of notice with a clear transition date and plan.

Here is a sample communication from a departing CEO of a public multinational company:

> Throughout my tenure as CEO, I have been engaged together with our board of directors and our succession committee in the issue of talent management and succession. We are confident that <new CEO-elect> is prepared for his/her new responsibilities and is the best leader to direct our company into the future. One of our top priorities has been developing the next generation of leaders. We believe that <new CEO-elect's> appointment exemplifies in action our commitment to leadership development. Having worked closely with the CEO-elect for many years, I can attest to his/her

strategic vision and inspirational leadership and I am confident he/she will guide the company into the next phase of growth so that we will continue to win in the marketplace. I will be retiring from my role as CEO yet will stay on as an advisor to the company, focusing on customer service excellence.

Typically this type of announcement is followed by a press release that includes a biography of the new CEO and an endorsement by members of the board. A nice touch is for the departing CEO to provide a quotation affirming the new CEO's leadership ability and culture fit.

The major drawback of an early announcement is that the up-and-coming CEO is expected to act as the new CEO before having the full power of the role. Unhealthy behavior can creep in if all parties are not fully committed to supporting each other and a professional transition. When people act with dignity and maturity and put the best interests of the company and each other at the top of their priority list, the transition typically works out well. (But be warned: it can be easier said than done!)

Announce It at the Last Minute

Another common approach is to keep the name of the newly promoted CEO confidential until the very last minute. Jack Welch of General Electric was famous for this. The main advantage here is keeping CEO candidates focused on adding value: after all, they just might get the top job. With this approach, the CEO candidates are told who will be the next CEO right before the announcement is made (the night before, according to Welch), and immediately afterward everyone is expected to move into action. Of course, the downside is shell shock, with the unsuccessful candidates having to congratulate the new CEO while still licking their wounds.

Political Pitfalls

The Politics of Winners and Losers in the Selection Process

When people compete for the CEO job and lose out, it can hurt. This occurs for a number of reasons. First, competitive people don't like to lose; they strive to win. Flip the script here: how would you feel in this scenario?

Secondly, a fundamental human need is to have some control over one's destiny. When people lose a competition, it can feel as if a choice was "taken from them," which is not a good feeling for someone who likes to take charge and make things happen at work and in life.

Thirdly, losing can lead to affective forecasting—that miserable feeling where you feel down in the dumps and you fear you will stay there *forever*. According to a 2015 article by Heidi Halvorson and Dave Rock, affective forecasting is a cognitive bias that involves: "Judging your future emotional state based on how you feel now." Essentially, rejection hurts.

The good news is that you can ease the pain of rejection for candidates with a good dose of emotional intelligence. If you were rejected for an opportunity that mattered to you, wouldn't you feel better if someone took the time to have a reset conversation with you? And they helped you figure out what's next as new information became available?

One CEO we interviewed, who is known for creating highly admired corporate cultures, offered an enlightening point of view on how emotional intelligence can help in this scenario. He affirmed that there will inevitably be a winner and losers with CEO selection, but that losing candidates don't need to *feel* this way. When selecting a CEO, he wants each candidate, regardless of the outcome, to feel valued and appreciated for being important to the long-term success of the company. Notably, when the board appointed a new CEO to replace him, every single one of the candidates stayed with the organization.

When choosing his successor, this CEO was firmly committed to fostering a winning feeling in each of the candidates. As part of the selection phase, he put each candidate through a high-profile and rigorous selection process which included a personalized discussion with him about the respective candidate's strengths and limitations for the role. He made it clear that no CEO candidate was perfect and that the most successful leaders design careers around their personal strengths, while facing their weaknesses enables them to build a complementary team.

Once the CEO selection decision was made by the board, he sat down with each candidate and told them:

> You were part of this process because I believe in your potential. Although you didn't get the job, I know you are an important part of the company's future. I'll be your advocate. Can we discuss how to work with the incoming CEO to craft a role in this organization that uses your strengths and expands your contribution?

Using input from the outgoing and incoming CEO, each candidate received a customized development plan and, whenever possible, their job scope was adjusted. They all stayed with the business; the company continued to grow and was later sold at one of the highest valuations in its industry—ever.

We admire this CEO's approach because, as executive coaches, we have an inside view of what this win-lose dynamic is like for candidates. We coach candidates when they are trying to process their disappointment and what it means to them. There's a lot of defensive self-talk during this process. Often the self-talk starts out self-berating: "What did I do wrong?" "Why didn't I make it?" And then it becomes self-protective: "Don't they see how good I am?" When candidates feel undervalued or underappreciated, this can trigger a flight response, leading to behavior that is hard to understand logically, but leads to behaviours like taking unsolicited calls from headhunters. This is when your transition—as well as that of the new CEO—gets much trickier.

How One CEO Resolved a Turf War between the CEO-Elect and the New COO

One of our clients is the CEO of a hospitality company with a stellar reputation for developing people. He had two strong internal candidates for the CEO role, but, as is typical, he could only hire one. When he announced who would be promoted, politics started to bubble. The closer it came to transition time, the more competitive the two candidates became. The CEO-elect started posturing and the VP of Operations (the other candidate) rebelled. Rumors started that they were bad-mouthing each other to peers, much to the disappointment of the departing CEO.

Despite the candidates' behavior, the departing CEO believed that at the core they respected each other. His plan to nip their unproductive behavior? He sent the two men to the Super Bowl.

Seriously. He bought two tickets to the Super Bowl and told the candidates to go have a good time, with one condition: he wanted them to come back with a plan for how they were going to work together as their roles changed. He told them, "I want you to duke it out. Put everything on the table and come back and tell me honestly if you can work together as a team."

And they did. They came back with a set of agreements they could both get behind. One of their agreements that was notable was surrounding a key message. They agreed to tell employees that although only one of them was promoted to CEO, the reality is that they are a team. To them, it didn't matter about the formal reporting structure, even though only one of them would be CEO. Truth be told, they would both be comfortable working for each other because they respect each other and know they can't run the company alone.

Kudos to the departing CEO—politics averted. Expectations were made clear, agreements were made and the odds of success improved.

✓ In Summary

Carefully structure the selection process to minimize the likelihood of losing high-potential people who were not selected. Be transparent about the expectations for the individual being promoted to CEO and clarify the respective roles of the current CEO, board chair, board committee and human resources personnel in order to avoid missteps. Be thoughtful in negotiations with candidates, as these are delicate conversations that can have a lasting impact well after selection.

Pay close attention to your communication with the successful and especially the unsuccessful candidates. These conversations can set the tone for the incoming CEO. Set up the new CEO for success: prior to the handover, make the tough decisions that you've avoided. Show confidence by making verbal, visible or other signals that the incoming CEO has assumed the role and you have moved on. These actions send powerful messages through the company.

Recognize the domino effect of changes throughout the organization and strategically plan them as part of the overall process. Below are some self-coaching questions you can use to help you navigate this part of your journey, which can be very emotional and stressful.

? **Self-Coaching Questions**

- What kind of support do you wish you had when you last transitioned into a CEO role? Given this, what do you want to put in place for the incoming leader?

- What can you do to show confidence in the CEO-elect? Any symbolic gestures come to mind?

- Are you prepared for the day when the new CEO is announced? What will your first action be?

- What are you avoiding?

- If you decide to stay on as board chair or board member or in another capacity, ask yourself the following questions:

  - Am I staying on to defer my own personal decision about my next career move?

  - If I really have confidence in the new CEO and have gone through a proper introductory session and transfer of corporate memory, what real value will I be adding if I stay on?

  - Given my personality and style, could I be more helpful to the incoming CEO as an external advisor, without the fiduciary duties and history of leading the company?

6

BE
SELF-AWARE:
LET GO AND
MOVE ON

Key Leadership Quality

Be self-aware. Let go and move on. Be aware of your deeply felt emotions. Resist the urge to fill the void quickly.

Toward the end of my transition, I felt so recognized and appreciated that I ignored the emotional cliff I was walking toward. The day after I changed my title to "former CEO" and the constant e-mails and meetings stopped, I suddenly felt like I went from being a somebody to a nobody.

THE NEW CEO has taken over. Now what? When the transition is done, you may be tempted to jump to the next thing to fill the void without thinking much about what you truly want. But this is the time to stop and reflect and ask yourself some important questions: What do you really want to do next? What matters to you now?

As a past CEO you likely have your material needs met, so these questions aren't necessarily about economics and material gain; they are more existential. What would you find *meaningful* to pursue? What would feel *significant* for you? After transitioning out of your role, you have an opportunity to pause and think about how to reorient your life and spend your time.

One thing that gets in the way of carving out time to reflect is the "success blueprint" imprinted on CEOs: set a vision, take swift action and be decisive. Although this paradigm creates success in the CEO job, it can create problems when transitioning *out of the job*. In this phase, you need to let go of some of the intensity and urgency that makes you successful as a CEO. Defining your next phase is not something you can think your way out of: you need space to break some of your old patterns and engage in a process of self-discovery. It takes time to consider what will re-invigorate you in meaningful ways.

Notwithstanding whether you want another CEO job, full retirement without work or a career reinvention, we have some tools and insights to help you gain clarity about what's important to you. However, in our opinion, you can learn best from what the CEOs we interviewed have to say about their transitions. Hearing about the actual experiences of other individuals in similar circumstances won't tell you what to do, but it will provide you with an arsenal of insights and techniques with which to tackle your own situation.

⬛ What Successful CEOs Do

Align Future Career Options with Your Values

Being a CEO can shape your values in ways you might not even be aware of. It's common for us to pick up values from the circumstances we find ourselves in. Just think about growing up with your parents and how long it took you to define your life on your own terms. Now is the time to do a values reset and to figure out what matters to you in this new career and life phase. Here the question is no longer "What does success mean to me?"; it's "I have achieved success, now what?"

One CEO reflected: "I didn't realize what a privilege it was to be a CEO until I was no longer in the job." When he left, he went through a period of mourning. He recalled one incident when, after having retired from that job, he took a flight and no longer had elite status giving him privileges on an airline. He thought to himself, "What have I become?" Thankfully he could laugh at himself and he didn't have a knee-jerk reaction. He boarded the plane, took an extended vacation and stayed committed to designing his life and career around his own values, re-orienting his identity in the process.

As a longtime leader, you know that designing your life around your life *and* career is a wise approach. No matter what your age, you're likely at a point where you realize life is finite. Your burning question in self-reflection is likely: If not now, *when?* This can refer to a dream you had put on hold while pursuing a CEO role or a desire to contribute to your community, or it could be another CEO role. The choices are limitless.

As one CEO explained:

> I'm well aware that at this point the clock is ticking, so I am much more intentional about where I put my energy. Now, being intentional has a whole new dimension to it.

The good news is that you have more options than ever before. Thanks to lifestyle advances, you probably have more energy than CEOs in similar positions had a decade or so ago. In the past, there was a traditional post-CEO career path— retire from your role, join a board of your past colleagues, play golf, travel and essentially coast. That is no longer the case. Many former CEOs we spoke with (and one of us— Brian) want something different. They want to capitalize on their lifelong experiences, knowledge, financial security and energy and to find ways to pursue interests and passions that got left behind as they met the demands of the CEO job.

Consider some of the things that former CEOs we know are doing today: writing, sharing their passion for identifying company values, coaching others to build their leadership skills, volunteering their time and talents, leading boards, focusing on being a grandparent or a better spouse, putting more energy into their spiritual side. In one case we know of, a senior person in a large organization shifted from being a managing partner to being an actor—a logical transition when you consider that as an executive you're acting a lot of the time anyway!

The point is, your work as CEO doesn't have to be the centerpiece of your life. If you intentionally design this new phase of your life, you may well find that transitioning *out* of the CEO job gives you as much opportunity for personal growth as when you transitioned *into* the job. As one CEO shared:

> When I first became a CEO, it was a time of intense personal development. I matured a lot as a person. The same can be said for when I transitioned out of the role. This time around I wasn't in my forties and trying to raise a family while my career skyrocketed, but it was equally significant and meaningful and it forced me to confront myself in a similar way.

View the Situation through a Career-Transition Lens

When you begin your transition journey, it's helpful to have a framework to use so you can pinpoint what stage of the transition you are in and what might be around the corner. This can normalize the experience and help you respond appropriately.

In their book *LifeLaunch: A Passionate Guide to the Rest of Your Life,* Pamela McLean and Frederic Hudson present a model of self- and career-renewal that they've honed over a decade of running career-transition workshops and training coaches in this area. Their model inspired our own development of a model—the 4R model—to capture the stages of CEO transition. As you read, we invite you to think about each stage and apply the model to your own experience, along with comparing your experience to that of other CEOs.

Recognize and Prepare for Four Transition Stages: The 4R Model

As a starting point, it's valuable to understand that career and life transitions go through four stages which unfold in a predictable way. We believe the career-transition process for CEOs is made up of four stages—rewarding, reactive, retreating and renewal—which we refer to as the "4R" model.

Each stage is generally accompanied by certain emotions and experiences, and there are tasks that need to be completed before you move to the next stage. If you are in a transition, you will eventually go through all four stages (and for some, you may go through the cycle a few times), but there is a risk that you may get impatient and try to rush the process or you may get stuck in one stage, preventing you from moving on to the next in a productive and positive way.

Four "R"s of career transition

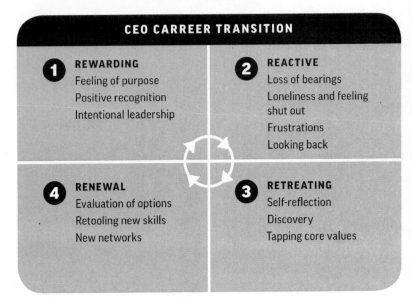

CEO CARREER TRANSITION

1 **REWARDING**
Feeling of purpose
Positive recognition
Intentional leadership

2 **REACTIVE**
Loss of bearings
Loneliness and feeling
shut out
Frustrations
Looking back

4 **RENEWAL**
Evaluation of options
Retooling new skills
New networks

3 **RETREATING**
Self-reflection
Discovery
Tapping core values

The Rewarding Stage

The rewarding stage is a time when you are in action mode, making your vision happen. You feel purposeful, energized and alive. Things align and flow. It's like the peak experience of being a CEO. When leaving the CEO job, our coaching clients tell us they worry they will never experience this rewarding feeling again and will be bored as a result. A CEO we spoke with explained:

> As a CEO there is a rhythm to your life as you strive to reach your goals—weekly team meetings, monthly

town halls, quarterly presentations and board meetings. It gives you a sense of purpose and a focus for your life.

As you start to move out of the CEO job, it's valuable to realize that although you will be out of the rewarding phase for a while, over time you will come back to it. Remember, too, that when you return to it, after working through the other stages, it will likely look and feel different. As Bob Burford, the author of *Halftime: Moving from Success to Significance*, says, "The first half of our life is about how to make a living. The second half is about how to make a life."

The Reactive Stage

The next stage can be like coming down after an adrenaline rush. Imagine retreating to a seaside cabin where you can hear the birds and see the rhythm of the waves. It's amazing at first, and then it can get a bit... quiet, especially for ex-CEOs. Some people feel as if they are floating without direction, unmoored or mired in a rut. For some the reactive stage is lonely. Others feel a sense of loss or regret. Some worry about the future. You may be confused and experience trepidation about the next step in your life, or you may hold tightly onto the past, wallowing in thoughts of business successes and missed friendships. Consequently, letting go may be a struggle.

You may think this stage will be different for you because there have been very few tough issues you couldn't solve in the past. Many CEOs we speak to and coach believed firmly that they were different from others only to find that they were kidding themselves; they indeed have the same feelings, aspirations and vulnerabilities as everyone else, tough as it is to admit it. Going through the reactive stage is part of the overall transition experience. You must accept that you can't go back to the way things were, so eventually you will need to change your focus and your script. If not now, when?

During the reactive stage, some people opt for a mini-transition like going on an extended holiday or they put a time limit on their period of self-reflection to help them manage their energy and worries. Others push toward action to avoid feeling uncomfortable. We appreciated the honesty of one CEO who described his reactivity this way:

> When I look back on my CEO career, I realize that half the time I was too revved up about stuff. I didn't need to be so amped—it didn't make me a better leader. When I started this transition, I noticed I was doing the same thing. My instinct was to be reactive, to push myself for results and to figure things out quickly. I soon realized that this time I needed to be more calm, so I refused to let the hyper energy overshadow my experience.

Another CEO, who eventually embraced the reactive stage, said:

> As a CEO my life was so busy that I felt like ninety percent of my time was managing logistics. Come Sunday morning, I was already planning for the week ahead and preparing myself for what was to come. When I left the CEO job, it was as if time stopped. I felt very

uncomfortable! I soon learned it was a time to be more reflective, to sit back and observe; not a time to act impulsively, jumping in and starting to build things right away. When I thought about it, I often advised my team to be patient when proposing investments and acquisitions. It's so much easier to advise others than to do it yourself!

The Retreating Stage

When the reactivity slows and you begin to settle down, you detach from the past chapter of your life and begin to take time out to reflect. You are entering the retreating stage. Typically in this stage you take stock of your life, create a new conversation with yourself and tap into your core values.

To get the most from this stage, you need to disengage from your old life to some extent. You need time for *being* yourself, not just *doing* your job, which can be difficult for type-A, action-oriented CEOs. Suspend the urge to act. Find time to relax, and work through your inner desires, hopes and dreams. It usually takes a few months or more to move through this stage properly. Our message is don't rush through this important stage of your transition or the void you are trying to fill might not only remain; it could get bigger.

One CEO asked himself some difficult questions:

I have been so focused on my work up until this point in my life, and I can honestly say that I achieved a level of success in my career that exceeded my expectations. But this focus caused me to leave other things off the table. At this point in my life I need to go back and pick up some pieces and really delve a bit deeper into the inner corners of my being. How is my ego getting in the way of what I really want in life? Why do I tend to hold back when it comes time to express my true feelings? Why is it that my kid is so mad at me half the time? I think the answers to these questions will help prepare me for the rest of my life.

Another CEO used the retreating stage to re-craft his identity and figure out what truly mattered to him:

One question that was really helpful for me was: What part of my CEO identity did I want to stick with me after I leave the job? For me, the answer was my character. I didn't want to leave my character behind—the part of me that likes to deal with complex issues and collaborate with interesting people, and that cares about acting with high integrity and keeping my word.

On a similar note, a CEO who is now fully retired reflected:

So much of my identity was my job. I was CEO and everyone respected me. I travelled a lot to interesting places around the world in business class. I was doing many things and always on the run. I took some time away to ask myself: Who would you be if you lost it all? What kind of person would be left? My most honest answer was: I don't know. It took me some time to discover it for myself.

The Renewal Stage

Once you've taken the time to figure out what you want, you'll be ready to develop scenarios for yourself—to experiment, retrain, network and get ready for the next chapter that you've designed. In the renewal stage you may want to test ideas, try new things and develop new skills, and you may find that you need a dose of humility.

One of the CEOs we spoke to went into consulting in his "passion area"—culture. But doing so required him to learn how to be a consultant again, something that took some trial and error. Another CEO wanted to get on boards, but she realized that her core competency in technology was weak and that the kinds of companies she was interested in weren't as interested in her. A third CEO got on boards only to discover it wasn't as gratifying as he expected, and he wanted to be a CEO again.

Pursuing a values-oriented life of significance sometimes takes more courage than you might at first expect. You may know how to be a CEO but you fear falling flat on your face when you try something different, especially if your new pursuits are aligned more with dormant passions than with your honed business skills. It can be helpful to give yourself a set time frame for experimentation before putting pressure on yourself to make concrete plans and communicating a definite path to a broad network of people.

The CEOs we spoke with had a lot to share about what it was like to move into the renewal stage. Following are valuable observations from some of them:

- From my perspective, when I left my CEO job I had to come up with a new identity. I had to cycle through a few different options before I found one that fit me. I watched my wife go through something similar when she was an empty nester for the first time.

- At this point in my life I wanted to have some compelling life experiences that go beyond work. This whole idea of putting around on a golf course all the time doesn't appeal to me. The reality is that I am one of the lucky ones and I have enough money to do what I want. I want to pack a lot of living into this chapter.

- Somewhere along my journey, I realized that consumerism became a trap for me and my family. The first time I downsized my house, I was shocked by all the junk I had accumulated over the last fifteen years. I wanted this next chapter to be simpler and more about love and experiences and freedom, rather than acquiring more stuff I don't need or, frankly, even want anymore.

- At first I really wanted to stay on as the board chair, but after taking some time away, I changed my mind. I realized that I could play a better role as the new CEO's advocate if I was a director rather than the chair, and I had been with the company for so long, my pre-existing biases would get in the way. I started to consider other options. I experimented with speaking, taking on new projects and other things I always wanted to do.

- When I first met my wife, I found her company to be invigorating. She would challenge me and she had a different life from mine, so we would often chuckle about issues we disagreed on and it was entertaining to hear about each other's day. But after years of working day and night, I was worried about the thought of spending so much time together. We had to test out how much we could be together and still enjoy it!

Although the renewal stage can raise some challenging questions, it is primarily an exciting, forward-looking period. When this stage is over, it will be time to "go for it" and enter the rewarding stage once again. For many, the cycle will now begin anew.

Where Are You Now?

Before moving on to the next section of the book, take a minute to consider which of the four "R" stages you're in right now and what is to come for you. Are you moving through the stages at a productive pace and setting clear goals for yourself? Are you leading yourself through the stages with clear intent? Or are you rigid, trying to control things, denying your feelings, holding on tightly to the past or pushing yourself prematurely to certainty?

If you've moved through the four stages with intention, you will now be re-entering the rewarding stage. At this new stage of your career the rewards will be different than when you were selected as CEO, but it can still be a time of excitement and interesting personal growth.

Update Your Personal Narrative

The CEO stories we have shared illustrate how important it is to ask yourself key questions as you move through your career transition in order to gain a deeper understanding of what is important to you. One former CEO recalls:

> One challenge that exiting CEOs have is that they have so many people trying to tell them how they are going to be happy. No one told you how to be happy in the first place, you had to figure that out for yourself. It's the same for life after being CEO. You have to figure out what gets you up in the morning.

Your answers will help you weave a new narrative, perhaps with a new definition of success, appropriate to the next chapter of your life. As a CEO we interviewed said:

> You should think of your life and career like chapters of a compelling novel. What do you want this next chapter to be about? What's the plot, the narrative? And what's important to the main character?

To help you redefine success on *your* transition journey, we've extracted questions from our interviews and from our work with CEOs during their respective transitions. We hope you take the time to ask yourself these questions so that you can create your own storyline around what's important to you at this stage, what's missing and what you need to express to be fulfilled. When you do this, you will resist the temptation to keep doing what you're doing now and to hang on too long. You will avoid becoming one of those CEOs who bumble around the office unsure of what to do with themselves. No one wants that.

Preparing Your New Narrative: Some Starter Questions

1. What does success mean to you now? What do you really want at this life stage?

2. When you imagine your eightieth birthday, what will be important to you then?

3. What do you enjoy doing and want to do more of? How often is doing these activities enough for you?

4. What part of you did you leave off the table in order to pursue a CEO role? What are the unmet needs that were not satisfied?

5. What brings a sense of meaning and purpose to your life?

6. Which parts of the CEO lifestyle were gratifying and fulfilling? Which parts did you like best and would ideally like to have in your life in some continued way?

7. Which aspects of being a CEO did you find unfulfilling or even punishing? What are the parts you want to eliminate as you move forward?

8 What kind of contribution do you still want to make in the world?

9 What are the ways you can pay it forward or express gratitude for your good fortune in life?

10 What constraints or limitations do you need to consider?

Throughout this book we have shared personal stories from individuals we interviewed and have kept their identity anonymous. Here, to inspire your new narrative, Brian tells his own story of CEO transition and reinvention:

After a highly fulfilling career in a firm with a family-like atmosphere, it was naturally hard for me to leave—very hard. After thirty-four years in the company, including nine as the regional president of the Canadian operations, and the last six as Global President and CEO, I had achieved success beyond my dreams. I have many fond memories of being involved with talented people as the company grew from a small, and largely unknown, regional player to a recognized global powerhouse. And there were also challenging times, the ups and downs that come with business cycles. I thought this broad experience made me battle-tested for almost anything, including my transition; however, it did not. Why?

My rational side said it was appropriate to step aside and let the next generation of leaders guide the firm to its next horizon. After all, the firm had always done that in the past. I worked with the board on a sensible transition period, yet I still found it difficult personally. I didn't want to leave the adrenaline-filled job of the CEO. Also, I didn't want to lose the comfort of being surrounded by many friends, my routines, my support systems and my business connections.

While the recognition dinners and so many e-mails and cards of thanks and good wishes I received during the final months of my transition allowed me to hold on to the good memories, it had to end. Then reality hit, and it hit hard. I'd entered a dark, cold place that I dreaded—the reactive stage. The constant e-mails, travel and meetings had ended, and I lost all the support systems I had taken for granted. This seemingly happened cold turkey! I knew that it was coming, but I didn't realize how difficult it was going to be. People didn't return my calls or e-mails as quickly as before, and sometimes not at all!

Intellectually I knew that, previously, people were responding to the CEO position more than to me personally, but I thought I was different—my ego got in the way and I was reactive. I wanted to quickly build something to fill that void. I told myself it was time to "suck it up and move on," a tactic I had used in business for many years. But upon reflection, I first had to test my new narrative and reflect on my values and personal goals. This was my transition to the reflective stage, which lasted for a while.

While I was President/CEO I was often asked, "What will you do after the CEO job?" I had a narrative constructed in my mind (in retrospect, I should have written it down). I was consistent in my goals to continue to help executives grow their leadership skills, contribute to boards, volunteer and share my knowledge. Now it was time to actually do it. After taking some time to retreat and reflect, I knew this is where I could make the biggest contribution to others and be highly fulfilled personally. Time to reinvent.

Now I won't shy away from acknowledging the challenge of this shift and the time I needed to retreat and reflect. Honestly, while I tried to convince myself otherwise at the time, it was a very big shift. I had to slow down—something I was not used to doing. As I look back, this reflection period was good for me. I was encouraged by my family and former executive coach (who remains a close friend today) to pursue my passions.

So I enrolled in a training course for executive coaching. That was an experience—hanging out with young people, most of whom were women from the HR field who were accustomed to showing their emotions. Next, I completed the Directors Education Program at the Institute of Corporate Directors and obtained the ICD.D designation. This time, I was hanging out with colleagues more around my age and level of professional experience—much more comfortable.

What I learned from these experiences was that moving out of my comfort zone was necessary and provided the greatest opportunity for real personal growth. I started doing executive coaching and business advisory work on a pro bono basis, then started to get coaching and other business clients, and it began to build.

Today I'm engaged as much as I want to be with a diverse roster of executives whom I coach and mentor, I sit on some great boards and I'm working with many organizations and leading industry peer groups. And I'm working on this book! Now that is something I had not dreamed of doing, which turned out to be a wonderful experience to learn and grow and work with talented people like Natalie. All of this to say, I'm having fun.

The biggest lesson I would share from my journey so far is to listen to your head *and* your heart. Take the time to reflect, and don't jump too quickly into new things. If you reinvent yourself, don't expect to measure success as you did in the past. As a former CEO, you already have a lot to offer, and I can tell you from personal experience that people out there are just waiting for you to arrive.

As you update your narrative and move through your transition, remember it is a process, not a destination. Whatever you have achieved until now will help you lay the foundation for what is next. You have a fresh chance to do things not because you are competent at them, but because they bring new threads of meaning into your life.

Our hope is that your next chapter will last longer and be more energetic and vibrant than earlier generations of CEOs could ever imagine. Onward and upward!

 **In Summary**

One thing is for certain—every CEO will leave their job and company at some point; it's a matter of when. So ask yourself: if this CEO job ended today what would I want to do next? If you decide to remain in the business in a different role, consider whether it's the right thing for the company, for the new CEO and for you. Reflect back to when you were appointed and ask yourself if you would have wanted the former CEO to be actively involved.

Recognize that you will go through all four career-transition stages. The rewarding stage teems with accolades and excitement as you are the recently departed ex-CEO. You receive recognition dinners and calls of good wishes; you reflect positively on your legacy with great satisfaction. This stage will end. If you are like many others we have spoken with, you will want to fill the emotional gap quickly—the reactive stage. Our advice is to control those feelings. Allow yourself to experience a period of self-examination in the retreating stage when you begin to discover what you really want to do and where you will find happiness and meaning. This is a time to be reflective and contemplative. We caution you to be patient as you go through the stages; you may even go through the entire four-stage cycle more than once. Don't prejudge what you think will be rewarding for you before stepping down. Your priorities and needs will have changed. Take the time to update your personal narrative and to revisit it often, so that you're prepared for the continued questions about what is next from friends and colleagues. Follow your new passions—the renewal stage—as you retool. Refocus and begin to contribute to new areas that bring you meaning. And finally, don't let your ego get in the way of planning for your transition by inducing you to try to skip a stage. You are probably not different from everyone else.

Leaving any job can be a challenge. Leaving the top job as CEO is most often an emotionally charged journey to be experienced with patience without trying to force things to a rapid conclusion. As in many things in life, time is a great healer. Reflect on the leadership styles you used throughout your career to tackle challenging tasks and think of the advice you offered to others who were experiencing career transitions (even the ones that you initiated for them!). Recognize that you have the tools and experience to get through your own transition as well.

When the moment arrives, letting go and moving on can seem like a mountain to climb, and you may feel unprepared to tackle it. The following self-coaching questions may help you prepare and navigate the journey with a positive mindset.

? Self-Coaching Questions

- If you want to stay on after your transition, what motivates you to feel that way? Would you have wanted the former CEO to stay on and be active when you were appointed?

- As you consider the four stages of transition, which one do you think will be the most challenging for you?

- What values would you like to honor in your transition planning?

- Which things did you suspend or minimize while being CEO that you would like to pursue now?

- You will be asked how you are spending your time after you leave the CEO job; with this in mind, have you updated your personal narrative so you can respond confidently?

CONCLUSION: FROM SUCCESS TO SIGNIFICANCE

When I first started my career, I viewed myself like a mountain climber who takes on Mount Everest. I wanted to be the first to the top, the one to place the flag at the summit. Taking risks, getting prepared and working harder than everyone else got me to the top. At this stage in my career, I view things differently. I now want to be more like the Sherpa—guiding others to be successful on the journey because I know the path, watching with pride as they take in their view from the top.

N THE end, we hope this succession playbook inspires you to take on a more expansive view of a CEO transition, the antithesis of the short-term results mindset entrenched and pervasive in many companies.

In the truest sense, we hope the pragmatic insights we have shared, along with the process and toolkit, remind you that your CEO transition is as much about how you lead as following a structured process. It is unequivocally about planting seeds for the future (for others and for yourself) and about relationships. At its core it represents a shift in mindset from short-term success to longer-term significance.

To be blunt, our definition of hell is being on your deathbed looking back on life and seeing all the things you could have done and could have been in your life—all the opportunities for making a meaningful difference you somehow missed. You were too distracted, too busy or focused on other things. Our hope is that you read this book and take action by getting your own career vision sorted out, leading you to pursue the things you value most in your current life stage, so that you don't have any regrets.

We also hope that you lead your CEO transition clearly focused on developing others, so that in the end everyone involved wins and your business thrives long after you walk out the door—a long-term runaway success.

Need a little incentive to get started?

As a special bonus, on the companion website to this book (www.YourCEOSuccessionPlaybook.com) you'll find the following tools that will help you get started:

1. An overview of the CEO transition process for you and your board.
2. A printable career-coaching tool you can use with your high-potential executives to have meaningful dialogue about their career.
3. A leadership compass you can use for yourself, and others, as a way to identify what is most important to you right now.

Appendix

CEOs Interviewed

ANTHONY KARAKATSANIS, President and CEO, Morrison Hershfield Ltd., Toronto, ON

BOB CARD, former President and CEO, SNC-Lavalin Group Inc., Montreal, QC

BRIAN TIESZEN, former CEO, Sun Rich Fresh Foods Inc., Vancouver, BC

BRUCE BODDEN, former President and CEO, MMM Group (became part of WSP Global Inc.), Toronto, ON

CATHERINE ROOME, President and CEO, BC Safety Authority, Vancouver, BC

CYNTHIA JOHANSEN, Registrar and CEO, College of Registered Nurses of British Columbia, Vancouver, BC

DARRYL MATSON, Senior Vice President, Bridges, COWI North America (formerly Buckland & Taylor Consultants), Vancouver, BC

DAVE HUELSKAMP, President and CEO, Merrick & Company, Denver, CO

DEAN NOBLE, CEO, Gordon Food Service Canada, Toronto, ON

FLEMMING BLIGAARD PEDERSEN, former Group CEO, Ramboll Group A/S, Copenhagen, Denmark

FRANK GEIER, former President, Gordon Food Service Canada, Vancouver, BC

GARY KOMAR, President and Chair, Dillon Consulting Limited, Toronto, ON

JENS-PETER SAUL, Group CEO, Ramboll Group A/S, Copenhagen, Denmark

JIM BALFOUR, former President, Dillon Consulting Limited, Toronto, ON

JIM METCALFE, former Chief Executive, Cansult Limited (became AECOM Middle East), Toronto, ON

JIM MURRAY, Managing Partner, Brian Jessel BMW, Vancouver, BC

JOHN ROSE, Past President and CEO, Nuheat Industries Limited Inc. (became Pentair), Vancouver, BC

KEVIN MCELROY, Past President and CEO, Nuheat Industries Limited Inc. (became Pentair), Vancouver, BC

LEN MURRAY, President and CEO, Klohn Crippen Berger, Vancouver, BC

MO JESSA, President, Earls Restaurants, Vancouver, BC

NEIL CUMMING, former President, Levelton Consultants Ltd. (became part of WSP Inc.), Vancouver, BC

NEVILLE ISRAEL, President and CEO, Sun Rich Fresh Foods Inc., Vancouver, BC

RALPH CHRISTIE, former CEO, Merrick & Company, Denver, CO

RANDY BERTSCH, President, Island Savings, Victoria, BC

ROBERT GOMES, President and CEO, Stantec Inc., Edmonton, AB

ROD DEWAR, former President and CEO, Island Savings, Victoria, BC

RON WILSON, former President and CEO, Morrison Hershfield Limited, Toronto, ON

STAN FULLER, CEO, Earls Restaurants, Vancouver, BC

STEVEN HUNT, President and CEO, COWI North America, Inc., Vancouver, BC

TIM GITZEL, President and CEO, Cameco Corporation, Saskatoon, SK

TOM LAND, President and CEO, Ecowaste Industries Ltd., Vancouver, BC

TONY FRANCESCHINI, former President and CEO, Stantec Inc., Edmonton, AB

References and Recommended Further Readings

Aitken, David, Geordie Aitken, Kyle V. Davy, and R. Hoffman. *The Leadership Succession Lifecycle in Best-Practice Firms.* American Council of Engineering Companies, 2012.

Anterasian, Cathy, and Dayton Ogden. "Succession Planning: Strategies for Building the Pipeline." *NYSE: Corporate Governance Guide.* Spencer Stuart publication by White Page, 2014.

Barrett Values Centre. "Personal Values Assessment (PVA)." http://www.valuescentre.com/our-products/products-individuals/personal-values-assessment-pva.

Björnberg, Åsa, and Claudio Feser. "CEO Succession Starts with Developing Your Leaders." *McKinsey Quarterly,* May 2015.

Burford, Bob. *Halftime: Moving from Success to Significance.* Zondervan, 1994.

Caspar, Christian, and Michael Halbye. "Making the Most of the CEO's Last 100 Days." *McKinsey Quarterly,* January 2011.

Charan, Ram. "The Secrets of Great CEO Selection." *Harvard Business Review,* December 2016.

Ciampa, Dan, and David Dotlich. *Transitions at the Top: What Organizations Must Do to Make Sure New Leaders Succeed.* John Wiley & Sons, 2015.

Corporate Executive Board. "CEB High-Potential Solution." http://www.cebglobal.com/talent-management/high-potential/solution.html.

Covey, Stephen R., and Breck England. *The 3rd Alternative: Solving Life's Most Difficult Problems.* Simon & Schuster, 2011.

Dattner, Ben, and Tomas Chamorro-Premuzic. "A CEO's Personality Can Undermine Succession Planning." *Harvard Business Review,* September 2016.

Dychtwald, Ken. "The New Retirement Workscape: An Antidote to Aging." *The Huffington Post, The Blog,* June 5, 2014.

Eigenbrod, Rick. *What Happens When You Get What You Want? Success and the Challenge of Choice.* Candescence Media, 2014. Kindle edition.

Goldsmith, Marshall. *Succession: Are you Ready?* Harvard Business Press, 2009.

Goleman, Daniel, Richard Boyatzis, and Annie McKee. *Primal Leadership: Realizing the Power of Emotional Intelligence.* Harvard Business School Press, 2002.

Halvorson, Heidi Grant, and David Rock. "Beyond Bias." *Strategy+Business,* July 13, 2015.

Hartnell, Chad. "Differences in CEO Leadership Style, Company Culture Improve Firm Performance, Study Finds." *Journal of Applied Psychology,* July 2016.

Kimsey-House, Henry, Karen Kimsey-House, Philip Sandahl, and Laura Whitworth. *Co-Active Coaching: Changing Business, Transforming Lives.* 3rd ed. Nicholas Brealey Publishing, 2011.

Korn Ferry, the Chief Executive Institute. http://www.kornferry.com.

Larcker, David F., Stephen A. Miles, and Brian Tayan. "Seven Myths of CEO Succession." Stanford Graduate School of Business, March 19, 2014.

MacDougall, Andrew J. "CEO Succession Planning." Presentation at a breakfast session of the Institute of Corporate Directors, BC Chapter, October 6, 2015. See www.YourCEOSuccessionPlaybook.com.

———. "The Route to the Top and Company Performance in CEO Transition." Canadian Spencer Stuart Board Index, 2009. See www. YourCEOSuccessionPlaybook.com.

McLean, Pamela D., and Frederic M. Hudson. *LifeLaunch: A Passionate Guide to the Rest of Your Life.* 5th ed. Hudson Institute Press, 2011.

Owl, Fox & Dean. "The Personal Leadership Canvas." http://www. owlfoxdean.com/leadership-canvas.

Pasmore, William. "Are You Ready? 4 Keys to Becoming a CEO." White paper. Center for Creative Leadership, 2014. http://www.ccl.org/articles/white-papers/4-keys-becoming-ceo.

Peters, James. "The Seven CEOs—The Essential Purpose of Succession Management." Internal publication of the Korn Ferry Institute, 2014.

Redmond, Andrea and Patricia Crisafulli. "Contemplating Life After Being CEO: The 4 Rs of Making a Comeback." *Chief Executive Magazine,* July 2010.

Saporito, Thomas J. "Ten Key Dimensions of Effective CEO Succession." *Ivey Business Journal,* January/February 2013.

Smart, Geoff, and Randy Street. *Who: The A Method for Hiring.* Random House, 2008.

Smith, Audrey B., Richard S. Wellins, and Matthew J. Paese. *The CEO's Guide to: Talent Management; A Practical Approach for Building Leadership Capability.* Development Dimensions International, 2011–16.

Spector, Jon, and Ron Williams. "How to Groom Millennial Leaders to Be Your Next CEO." Fortune.com, January 9, 2017.

Stamoulis, Dean T., and Erika Mannion. "Making It to the Top: Nine Attributes that Differentiate CEOs." Russell Reynolds Associates.

Stanier, Michael Bungay. *The Coaching Habit: Say Less, Ask More and Change the Way You Lead Forever.* Box of Crayons Press, 2016.

Stevenson, Jane Edison, Kevin Cashman and Dave Heine. "Ensuring a Seamless Transition to CEO." *NACD Directorship Magazine,* September/October 2014. http://www.NACDonline.org.

Winsborough, David. "CEOs Aren't Like Us." Thought Leadership Resources article. Hogan Assessment Systems Inc., 2012. http://www.hoganassessments.com/thought-leadership.

Acknowledgements

WE WOULD like to acknowledge all of the people that helped, encouraged, supported and worked directly with us to develop and publish this book. Walt Sutton provided early encouragement and honest feedback about editorial needs and with an introduction to Gayle Evers of Evers (Realtimeedit.com). We would gladly recommend Gayle to any new author seeking clarity in communication and amazingly fast response time. We would like to acknowledge Oksana Richards for her editorial prowess and never ending support. The team at Page Two Strategies is excellent to deal with and provide valuable advice and direction throughout the challenging process of publication and sales. We would like to thank all of the CEOs, Board members, professional advisors, peer group chairs and other professionals who were so enthusiastic in their support of our original concepts for the book and for their continued encouragement and support.

Finally, we also want to thank you, the reader, for picking up this book. It is an important step toward our ultimate goal: to set you up for success, to give you hope that CEO transitions can go smoothly, to inspire you to be a better coach and to touch people's careers in a positive manner.

About the Authors

NATALIE MICHAEL has worked in private practice developing executives for the last fifteen years. Whether as an executive coach, CEO forum chair or succession management consultant, her main goal is to help companies identify and develop executive potential. She has coached hundreds of executives, from Canada to Africa to New Zealand, with clients ranging from *Fortune* 100 companies to entrepreneurial start-ups.

Before turning to coaching and consulting, Natalie led organizations that won accolades such as best-managed company, fastest-growing company and top employer. In her personal time, she loves quiet mornings on her mat and hitting the trails with her family.

BRIAN CONLIN is an executive coach, mentor, board member and business advisor who worked in employee-owned organizations for over thirty years. He personally went through a successful transition as the former CEO of Golder Associates, a professional services firm that grew during his leadership from a modest regional business to a global powerhouse with over nine thousand employees and $1.5 billion in annual revenue.

During his career, Brian has coached and supported the development of dozens of leaders. Today he coaches executives from small start-ups through to large, complex firms. He enjoys engaging with executives who dream big, want to succeed and care for others. A family man with two grown boys and a granddaughter, he enjoys volunteering for worthy causes, cycling and playing golf.